Grammar Sense

WORKBOOK

4

Laura Chamberlain

OXFORD

UNIVERSITY PRESS

OXFORD
UNIVERSITY PRESS

198 Madison Avenue
New York, NY 10016 USA

Great Clarendon Street
Oxford OX2 6DP England

Oxford New York

Auckland Bangkok Buenos Aires Cape Town Chennai
Dar es Salaam Delhi Hong Kong Istanbul Karachi Kolkata
Kuala Lumpur Madrid Melbourne Mexico City Mumbai
Nairobi São Paulo Shanghai Taipei Tokyo Toronto

OXFORD and OXFORD ENGLISH are registered trademarks of Oxford University Press.

Editorial Director: Sally Yagan
Publishing Manager: Kenna Bourke
Associate Editor: Scott Allan Wallick
Production Manager: Shanta Persaud
Production Controller: Zai Jawat Ali

ISBN: 978 0 19 449020 7

10 9 8 7 6 5 4 3 2 1

Printed in Hong Kong

Contents

1 The Present

FORM, MEANING, AND USE

1 Examining Form

Read this student essay and complete the tasks below.

Language Influence

The use of the Spanish language in the United States <u>is growing</u> rapidly, and its influence <u>is</u> evident throughout the country. The widespread use of Spanish is no longer limited to New York, Florida, Texas, and California. In recent years, the use of Spanish <u>has been spreading</u> further into the interior of the country. Spanish <u>has become</u> important in states such as Utah, Michigan, and North Carolina, for example. In an effort to appeal to all of these Spanish speakers, companies are advertising in Spanish throughout the country, both on television and in print. Businesses of all kinds are striving to hire bilingual staff members to communicate with their Hispanic clients. Professionals in nearly every field are signing up for Spanish classes in order to expand their opportunities and earn more money.

Spanish has definitely changed life in the United States, but it is also clear that Spanish itself has been changing because of its close contact with English. Consider, for example, the many large bilingual communities that have been thriving all over the country. Because of the relationship between English and Spanish in these communities, many Spanish speakers have created Spanish words that come from English. For example, the word for "to have lunch" in Spanish is "almorzar," but many Spanish speakers in the U.S. prefer to use the word "lonchear." The traditional way to say "to park (the car)" in Spanish is "estacionar (el carro)," although in Miami you are more likely to hear the phrase "parquear (el carro)." This is an interesting time for the Spanish language in the United States. No one really knows what changes lie ahead for both the language and the country.

---

widespread: common; not limited to a particular area   **thriving:** becoming strong and successful
striving: trying

1. One example of the simple present, present continuous, present perfect, and present perfect continuous has been underlined. Find and circle more examples as follows::
   a. Three more examples of the simple present
   b. Three more examples of the present continuous
   c. Two more examples of the present perfect
   d. Two more examples of the present perfect continuous

2. Read the following sentence and check the correct statement below: "... the use of Spanish has been spreading further into the interior."

   _____ a. This action is ongoing.

   _____ b. This action has already been completed.

2 Contrasting Present Forms

Choose one or two correct phrases to complete each sentence.

1. He's never late. He _____ at eight o'clock every day.
   a. is picking me up   (b.) picks me up   (c.) has been picking me up

2. My children _____ with their friends right now.
   a. play   b. have played   c. are playing

3. José _____ Chinese for three years.
   a. is studying   b. studies   c. has been studying

4. According to the latest figures, millions of people in the United States _____ Spanish.
   a. speak   b. are speaking   c. have been speaking

5. Look at this ad in today's paper. The marketing department _____ a bilingual secretary.
   a. looks for   b. is looking for   c. has looked for

6. Rob _____ a journal since he was twelve years old.
   a. has kept   b. is keeping   c. has been keeping

7. The employees _____ a speech about diversity today.
   a. are listening to   b. listen to   c. have listened to

8. _____ my family in Mexico, but now it's time to go home.
   a. I visit   b. I've been visiting   c. I've visited

3 Answering Questions in the Present

Marc and Celia are married and both have full-time jobs. Look at the chart to see their schedules for today, then answer the questions.

TIME	MARC	CELIA
7:30-7:45 A.M.	Drive to work	Take the train to work
7:45-8:00 A.M.	Check e-mail	
8:00-8:30 A.M.	Attend a sales meeting	Check e-mail and voice mail
8:30-10:00 A.M.	Update all client information	Prepare budget reports
10:00-10:15 A.M.	Take a walk outside	Take a coffee break
10:15-12:00 P.M.	Meet with clients	Attend a budget meeting
12:00-1:00 P.M.	Have lunch with clients	Have lunch with coworkers
1:00-2:00 P.M.	Answer client e-mails	Analyze company spending data
2:00-2:30 P.M.	Research new houses available in the local real estate market	Continue analyzing company spending data
2:30-3:30 P.M.		Meet with company vice president
3:30-5:30 P.M.	Show homes to clients	Prepare spending analysis
5:30-5:45 P.M.	Drive home	Check e-mail
5:45-6:15 P.M.	Prepare dinner	Take the train home
6:15-7:00 P.M.	Eat dinner with Celia	Eat dinner with Marc

1. What does Marc do for a living?

    <u>He sells houses.</u>

2. Who works further from home, Celia or Mark?

    _____

3. It is 8:00 A.M. What has Marc already done today?

    _____

4. It is 9:30 A.M. What is Celia doing?

    _____

5. How long has Celia been doing this activity?

    _____

6. It is 1:30 P.M. What is Marc doing?

    _____

7. Who spends more time with clients, Celia or Marc?

    _____

8. Celia has just gone to lunch. What time is it now?

    _____

9. It is 6:30 P.M. What are Marc and Celia doing?

    _____

10. How long have they been doing this?

    _____

4) Completing Conversations in the Present

Complete these conversations using the simple present, present continuous, present perfect, or present perfect continuous form of the verbs in parentheses. More than one answer may be possible.

A. Malinda: Julie, <u>have you seen</u> (you/see) that new horror movie? Everyone _____ (say) it's
          ₁   ₂

          really great. I _____ (be) too busy to see it this week, but I really want to.
                          ₃

Julie: Oh no. I never _____ (watch) horror movies. They _____ (scare) me
                          ₄   ₅

          too much!

B. Derek: Hey, Akiko, _____ (be) you busy right now?
                          ₁

Akiko: Yes, I am. I _____ (write) a paper for my Italian class. It _____ (be)
                       ₂   ₃

          due tomorrow. I _____ (work) on it since 8:00 this morning!
                          ₄

C. Ali: I _____ (have) trouble deciding whether I should take German or Spanish this
             ₁

          semester. I _____ (want) to take German because I _____ (travel) to
                      ₂   ₃

          Germany three times and I really like it there. On the other hand, I _____ (know) I
                                                                               ₄

          will be able to use Spanish a lot here in the United States.

Scott: That's a tough decision. It sounds as if both will be useful to you. I _____ (study)
                                                                                 ₅

          Spanish for five years, and I _____ (think) it's a lot of fun.
                                        ₆

5 Thinking About Meaning and Use

Choose the correct response to each statement or question. There may be more than one correct answer for each.

1. "I've been studying in Florida for one month." The speaker . . .
   a. has completed his studies in Florida.
   b. is still studying in Florida.
   c. is making a general, timeless statement.

2. "The Spanish Club meets every other Friday at 2:00." The speaker is talking about . . .
   a. a habitual activity.
   b. an activity that is happening at the exact moment of speaking.
   c. how long an activity has been happening.

3. "How many people are learning Polish in Chicago these days?" The speaker wants to know about . . .
   a. something that is happening over an extended period of time.
   b. something that is changing.
   c. a completed activity.

4. "My brother has visited California three times." The speaker is talking about . . .
   a. a general truth.
   b. ongoing activities.
   c. a completed activity.

5. "What kind of work do you do?" The speaker wants to know about . . .
   a. a habitual activity.
   b. a state or condition.
   c. a temporary activity.

6. "I've been teaching English for seven years." The speaker is talking about . . .
   a. a state or condition.
   b. a completed activity.
   c. an ongoing activity.

6 Completing Sentences

Choose the best ending for each sentence below.

1. All day long I _____   A. have attended three concerts.

2. More and more people _____   B. have been sold out.

3. The past two exhibits _____   C. meets two nights each week.

4. This year we _____   D. have been thinking about you.

5. Our Japanese class _____   E. learn at different paces.

6. The students in my classes _____   F. are realizing the importance of foreign languages.

Find and correct the errors. The first one has been corrected for you.

Super Speaker Software

Are you interested in learning a second language? ~~Has~~ Have you been frustrated at your slow progress so far? Well, Super Speaker software is for you! Millions of students have tried our language learning software and they have been not disappointed. In conjunction with classroom learning, our software has helping students around the country learn a second language very quickly. Take Stephanie, for example. With our free demo, she reports that she has been learned Korean twice as fast! Our programs is available to learners of English, Spanish, French, Korean, Japanese, and Chinese. Another user, Ken, is a very busy man. He works full time, attends classes, and helping his mother take care of her house. He says our program has been a lifesaver! Similarly, Sasha is studying English, takes care of her children, and is looking for a job in the United States. Our program helps her focus on all her goals at once. She know she will find a job now that her English is improving so quickly. All of these customers have noticing a big difference in their language learning with Super Speaker software. They not been this satisfied with any other product. What you are waiting for? Order your free demo today!

Follow the instructions to write a descriptive paragraph. Use the Writing Checklist to check your work.

Think of one of your favorite activities and write some notes about it. What is the activity? Do you practice it alone or with others? Where and when do you practice it? How long have you been involved in the activity? How does it affect your life in general? List some of the reasons you like this activity. On a separate sheet of paper, use your notes to write a detailed paragraph describing the activity. Use the simple present, present continuous, present perfect, and present perfect continuous as appropriate.

Ever since I was a teenager, I have been practicing yoga. I feel relaxed whenever I do yoga either in a class or at home . . .

Writing Checklist

Reflect on your ability to use present tenses by answering the questions.

- [ ] 1. Did you use the present simple to describe general truths, routines, habits, or facts?
- [ ] 2. Did you use the present perfect to describe things that happened in the past and relate to the present?
- [ ] 3. Did you use the present continuous and/or the present perfect continuous to show changing situations?
- [ ] 4. Did you use time markers, such as *recently, up to now,* or *at the moment*?
- [ ] 5. Did you check your verb phrases for correct form?

---

2 The Past

FORM, MEANING, AND USE

1 **Examining Form**

Read this excerpt from a biographical novel and complete the tasks.

Prologue

Bob (was eating) dinner when it <u>happened</u>. He and his wife were talking about the weekend and the anchorman was reading the news on TV. At first, Bob and his wife weren't paying attention to the TV, but at 7:00 they tuned in to see the winning lottery numbers. Bob was thinking about what he would do with the eight million dollar jackpot, but he didn't really think he would win. The television reporter read the winning numbers and Bob heard his wife scream. He read the numbers on the TV screen, but he didn't believe what he saw. It couldn't be true! The winning lottery numbers he saw on the TV were the same numbers on the ticket in his wife's hand. Many thoughts were racing through Bob's mind. He knew his life would never be the same again.

Bob was right. His life changed that day. The day before, he and his wife had been living a normal life, but the lottery made them famous. Right away, Bob's friends were asking for money. Old acquaintances were calling him "just to catch up on old times." They pretended to be surprised when Bob told them about the lottery. He and his wife received many visitors, but they felt isolated from the world. Finally, they decided to move to a small island in the Caribbean, where nobody knew about the lottery. That is how Bob began the biggest adventure of his life.

---

anchorman: person on a news program who reads the news
lottery: a game where winners are chosen by chance
jackpot: the largest prize to be awarded in a game

1. Underline ten examples of simple past forms.

2. Circle seven examples of past continuous forms.

3. Find the one example of the past perfect continuous and circle it. How many auxiliary verbs are there? Check the correct answer.

   _____ a. One

   _____ b. Two

   _____ c. Three

2 Comparing the Past Perfect and the Past Perfect Continuous

A. Choose the correct words to complete each sentence.

1. She didn't eat lunch with us because she had . . .
   a. already been eating.
   b. already eaten. ⟨circled⟩

2. When the phone rang, . . .
   a. Teruo had been reading for three hours.
   b. Teruo had read for three hours.

3. When they rang the bell last night, I had . . .
   a. been sleeping soundly.
   b. slept soundly.

4. We ordered sushi although we had never . . .
   a. been tasting it.
   b. tasted it.

5. Brenda came to help me when I called even though she had . . .
   a. been watching her favorite television show.
   b. watched her favorite television show.

6. She was pleased because the package had finally . . .
   a. been arriving.
   b. arrived.

B. The following questions refer to the above activity. Put a check mark (✓) next to the correct answer.

1. The following questions refer to activity A.

   _____ a. past perfect

   _____ b. past perfect continuous

2. Why is that particular tense used in the clause?

   _____ a. It marks an earlier activity that was ongoing.

   _____ b. It marks an earlier activity that was already completed.

3 Working on the Present Perfect

Use the prompts in the box to write present perfect questions. Then write your own answer to each question. Use contractions when possible.

taste raw oysters	live in another country	eat catfish	get a promotion at
work	meet anyone famous	have an accident	run a marathon
make sushi	regret telling the truth	have an unusual job	quit a habit

1. Have you ever tasted raw oysters? No, I haven't. _____

2. _____

3. _____

4. _____

5. _____

6. _____

7. _____

8. _____

Complete this paragraph with the words in parentheses and the simple past, the past continuous, or the past perfect. In some sentences, more than one form is acceptable. Use contractions when possible.

You're not going to believe what ___happened___ (happen) to me yesterday! It _____ (be) a beautiful
                                        1   2

day and the sun _____ (shine). As I _____ (walk) home from work, a large dog suddenly
                      3   4

_____ (run) out from behind the bushes. I walk down this street every day, but I _____
      5   6

never _____ (see) this dog before yesterday. I _____ (be) really scared, because the big dog
                                                          7

_____ (bark) loudly. I _____ (not/see) its owner anywhere. The dog _____ (get)
      8   9   10

closer and I _____ (call) for help. Nobody _____ (come) to help me. I _____ (run)
                11   12   13

down the street, and the dog _____ (chase) me. I was sure he would attack me. But the strangest thing
                                  14

_____ (happen). When the dog finally _____ (catch up) to me, he _____ (not/bite)
      15   16   17

me. He just _____ (lie down) on the sidewalk and _____ (roll) on to his back, as though he
                18   19

wanted me to pet him! It was so strange!

Ana just got home from the first day of her new job. She is talking on the phone with her friend, Mario. Use the information in the schedule below to complete Mario's questions. Then write Ana's responses.

NEW EMPLOYEE TRAINING SCHEDULE

7:45 A.M.–8:00 A.M.	Coffee and social time. (Cafeteria)
8:10 A.M.–9:50 A.M.	President Smith's speech. (Meeting Room A)
10:00 A.M.–12:00 P.M.	Personnel meeting. Sign paperwork. (Green Room)
12:10 P.M.–1:30 P.M.	Lunch with marketing department. (Conference Room)
1:45 P.M.–3:00 P.M.	Computer training. (Meeting Room B)
3:15 P.M.–4:15 P.M.	Tour of company buildings. (Meet in Lobby)
4:30 P.M.–5:15 P.M.	Meet with immediate supervisor.

Ana: Hi Mario. How are you?

Mario: Good. I've been thinking about you all day. What time ____did____ you ____get____ (get) to
work today?

Ana: _I arrived at 7:45 A.M._

Mario: Wow! That's early. What _____ you _____ (do) next?

Ana: _____

Mario: Oh, I see. I called you at 1:00pm, but you didn't answer. What _____ you _____ (do)?

Ana: _____

Mario: _____ you already _____ (hear) President Smith's speech by that time?

Ana: _____

Mario: Oh, that's nice. What _____ (happen) after lunch?

Ana: _____

Mario: Oh, good. Working with computers can be tricky. _____ you _____ (get) a tour

of the company buildings?

Ana: _____

Mario: I'll bet that was interesting. You know, I thought you _____ (finish) work at 5:00 P.M., so I

called you at 5:05 P.M. _____ you still _____ (work)?

Ana: _____

Mario: Really? That sounds like a long day. What time _____ you _____ (leave) work?

Ana: _____

6 Thinking About Meaning and Use

Read each sentence and the statements that follow. Circle the correct statement for each. There may be
more than one correct answer for each.

1. "I've been to Mexico three times."
   a. The speaker is currently in Mexico.
   b. The speaker is talking about his past travels.
   c. The speaker's trip to Mexico was incomplete.

2. "I haven't eaten all day."
   a. The speaker is probably hungry.
   b. The speaker is probably full.
   c. The speaker hasn't been very busy today.

3. "Hiroko woke up when the phone rang."
   a. Hiroko was working when the phone rang.
   b. Hiroko was sleeping when the phone rang.
   c. Hiroko didn't hear the phone ring.

4. "What has Amy been doing all day?"
   The speaker wants to know . . .
   a. how Amy is feeling.
   b. the events of Amy's day.
   c. Amy's location.

5. Rachel drove to Chicago.
   a. Rachel arrived in Chicago.
   b. Rachel is still driving.
   c. Something interrupted Rachel on her way to Chicago.

6. Alberto was working when Jenny saw him.
   a. Jenny interrupted Alberto's work.
   b. Alberto had finished working before Jenny arrived.
   c. Alberto's work was ongoing when Jenny arrived.

Find and correct the errors. The first one has been corrected for you.

Spring Fashion Show

This year's Spring Fashion Show was the best ever. At 10:00 A.M., the models *were* ~~was~~ arriving and the photographers were taking pictures. The fans has been waiting in the streets for several hours. Everyone was cheered when the famous designers walking down the red carpet. All the spectators had taken their seats inside the theater when the show began. The models walk down the runway in the season's most beautiful new fashions.

Each model walked to the end of the runway and turned slowly so everyone could see the fashions clearly. The photographers was snapping pictures and the crowd were cheering enthusiastically throughout the entire show. The most popular designs of the season including bright colors and straight lines. Most of the designs been featured long flowing skirts and suits. The shirts was loose with long sleeves. They were the best creations the fashion world has ever seeing.

Follow the instructions to write a paragraph that describes an interesting event that happened in your past. Use the Writing Checklist to check your work.

Choose an interesting event that happened in your past. On a separate sheet of paper, jot down a few notes about the events that occurred. Use the simple past and the past perfect to show the sequence of completed past events. Use the past continuous and the past perfect continuous to describe what was in progress when the events happened.

I was driving home from work late at night and it was raining very hard. There were many parked cars near the side of the road, waiting for the storm to pass. I was in a hurry and decided to continue driving . . .

Writing Checklist

Reflect on your ability to use past tenses and shifts to present by answering the questions.

☐ 1. Did you use the simple past and the past perfect to show the sequence of two past situations?

☐ 2. Did you use the past continuous and the past perfect continuous to emphasize an activity that was ongoing?

☐ 3. Did you use time clauses?

☐ 4. Did you shift between past and present to support ideas or contrast information?

☐ 5. Did you use present tenses to make a general comment or explain something?

☐ 6. Did you check your verb phrases for correct form?

3 The Future

FORM, MEANING, AND USE

1 Examining Form

Read this travel advertisement and complete the tasks below.

JOIN US FOR A CRUISE IN THE SUNNY CARIBBEAN!

If you choose to join our trip, your vacation will begin with a one night stay in Miami. Your cruise leaves Miami at 6:00 a.m. on March 3 and remains at sea for six nights and seven days. While at sea, you will experience the finest food, entertainment, and lodging the Caribbean has to offer. Your stateroom will have an ocean view and a private bathroom. Prepare to feast on succulent food each evening in our Sunset Dining Room, where you will dine on the freshest fish and seafood. All passengers will enjoy our indoor pool and our three outdoor pools.

You are going to love our fitness programs. We offer water aerobics, spinning, and yoga classes. Join us for organized sporting events such as water volleyball. The Sunrise Deck hosts activities such as shuffleboard, mini golf, and jogging. Perhaps you'll have had enough sun by the end of the day. In that case, you'll head inside to watch our premiere live entertainment. You will also be able to take dancing lessons, go bowling, or enjoy our bars and dance clubs. Sound like fun? Well, after doing all this you still won't have left the ship! But by the end of your cruise, you will have visited beautiful Puerto Rico, the fabulous Bahamas, and the ever popular Grand Cayman Island. You won't find a vacation like this anywhere else, so join us for our cruise in the sunny Caribbean!

---

succulent: tasty, delicious
shuffleboard: a game in which players use a long pole to push disks toward a goal
premiere: first, best in quality

1. Circle seven examples of the simple future.

2. Underline two examples of the future perfect and one example of the future with *be going to*.

3. Find the sentence containing two examples of the simple present as future and underline it. Why did the writer use the simple present as future? Check the correct answer.

    _____ a. The sentences express a quick decision.

    _____ b. The sentences refer to something scheduled.

2 Contrasting Future Forms

Choose one, two, or three correct phrases to complete each sentence.

1. I can't help you tomorrow because _____.
   a. I will visit a friend   (b.) I'm going to visit a friend   c. I visit a friend

2. By this time next year, we _____ for three months.
   a. will have been married   b. will have married   c. are marrying

3. _____ a long line at the ticket counter. You can expect to wait.
   a. There's going to be   b. There will be   c. There'll have been

4. Here's the course schedule. Next week _____ more about chemical reactions.
   a. they're learning   b. they're going to learn   c. they learn

5. Watch out! That car _____ us!
   a. is going to hit   b. will hit   c. hits

6. The students _____ late today due to the bad weather.
   a. will be arriving   b. will have been arriving   c. are going to be arriving

7. _____ for an hour by the time you get here.
   a. I'll have been working   b. I am working   c. I'll have worked

8. Rob's mother _____ in two weeks.
   a. is arriving   b. is going to arrive   c. arrives

3 Practicing Future Forms

A. Mr. Ajani is a candidate for mayor of his town. Read the statements made by the candidate and his aides. Then match the statements to the descriptions below.
   a. **Mr. Ajani:** One thing I'm certain about, I won't allow developers to change our town.
   b. **Press Secretary:** A few announcements. The first of three town hall meetings begins tonight at 7.
   c. **Fund Raiser:** Because of campaign finance reform, future campaigns will be much different than the current one.
   d. **Campaign Manager:** The candidate is going to rest and relax this weekend.
   e. **Assistant 1:** Look at this poll. Mr. Ajani is going to be thrilled!
   f **Assistant 2:** There's a problem with the campaign bus. I'll go see what's going on.
   _____ a scheduled event that is unlikely to change
   _____ a prediction about the immediate future based on evidence
   _____ an informal plan that could change
   _____ a more distant prediction
   _____ a promise
   _____ a quick decision

B. Now write:
   1. one more campaign promise

   _____

   2. one more campaign prediction

   _____

   3. one more scheduled campaign event

   _____

   4. one more informal campaign plan

   _____

4 Thinking About Meaning and Use

A. Read these sentences and complete the tasks below.

1. You can stop doing the dishes and go get ready. I'll do the dishes for you.
2. I'm probably going to travel with my cousin this summer.
3. I think someday humans will live on the moon.
4. When you're in class, I'll probably be waiting in the car if I can't find parking.
5. The drug store opens at 7:00 in the morning.
6. I bet you're going to find a job this week.
7. Joe's going to Honduras to see the Mayan ruins in March.
8. Class begins at 1:15.
9. I think a lot of people are going to be buying houses this year.
10. I wonder how my sister is feeling. I'll call her right now.

B. Complete the following tasks based on the sentences above.

a. Find two examples of planned future activities. Which one is a more definite plan?

_____

b. Find two examples of a quick decision.

_____

c. Find two examples of predictions about future activities or states.

_____

d. Find two examples of predictions about future activities in progress.

_____

e. Find two examples of scheduled activities.

_____

5 Responding to Questions About the Future

Choose the best response for each question or statement below.

_____ 1. Do you want my help when I arrive?

_____ 2. What are you doing today at 3:00?

_____ 3. When should I plan to see you?

_____ 4. Do you have any vacations planned?

_____ 5. You don't spend enough time with your brother.

_____ 6. Oh, no! I'll never finish on time!

A. I'll be working.

B. My train arrives at noon.

C. I'm going to Rome next month.

D. Don't worry. I'll help you.

E. Well, I'm going to see him later today.

F. No, I'll have finished everything by then.

6 Practicing the Future Perfect

Satomi is flying to Costa Rica. Her friends are looking at her itinerary. Complete the sentences according to Satomi's schedule. Use the future perfect and future perfect continuous.

1:00 P.M. – Call to confirm flights	**5:00 P.M. – Board airplane**
2:45 P.M. – Arrive at airport	**5:30 P.M. – Plane leaves for San Jose**
3:00 P.M. – Get boarding passes	**12:00-4:30 A.M. – Ride to university**
3:15 P.M. – Check baggage	**4:45 A.M. – Arrive at hotel**
4:00 P.M.– Pass through security	

1. By the time Satomi arrives at the airport, she _will have confirmed her flights_____.

2. Satomi _____ by the time she checks her baggage.

3. There's a lot of security at the airport these days. By the time Satomi passes through security, she _____.

4. I'm going to bed at 11:00 tonight. By that time, Satomi _____ for San Jose.

5. By the time we wake up tomorrow morning, Satomi _____ at her hotel.

6. When Satomi arrives at her hotel, she _____ for almost 14 hours!

7 Using Future Forms

Read the following pairs of sentences. Write *S* if the sentences have the same meaning. Write *D* if their meanings are different. For the sentences that are different, change the *b* sentence so that it means the same as *a*.

___D___ 1. **a.** There will be a lot of people at the meeting tonight.

           b. There are a lot of people at the meeting tonight.

           There are going to be a lot of people at the meeting tonight.

_____ 2. **a.** We have to hurry. The store is going to close at 10:00.

           b. We have to hurry. The store closes at 10:00.

_____

_____ 3. **a.** We will be happy if this business is a success.

           b. We are happy if this business is a success.

_____

_____ 4. **a.** We'll be taking flying lessons in Texas next month.

           b. We're taking flying lessons in Texas next month.

_____

_____ 5. **a.** Jake will help us with the projects.

           b. Jake helps us with the projects.

_____

_____ 6. **a.** Be careful! You'll be driving on a dangerous road.

           b. Be careful! You're going to drive on a dangerous road.

_____

8 Editing

Find and correct the errors. The first one has been corrected for you.

FIGHTING FOR THE FUTURE OF OUR HISTORY

Our town has a reputation for preserving our historic buildings. Thanks to the efforts of concerned citizens, our grandchildren will ~~enjoying~~ *enjoy* Main Street's historic storefronts and many other important landmarks. In the past thirty years, our citizens have worked hard to save our history for future generations. One of our lesser-known historic buildings is currently being threatened, however, by new development. If citizens do not act, we will going to lose a very important building in our city's landscape. A company called Knox Developing is going to have purchase the Morton Building with plans to knock it down. The Morton Building will has vanished within a few months unless we can stop the purchase. According to Marty Rogers, Smithfield Historic Preservation Council chairman, the council are going to try and have the building added to the National Register of Historic Places. "We is going to speak to the judge and requested a court order to halt demolition of the building. We are organize large groups of concerned citizens to protest when Knox Developing will arrive at the site. We will let the developer know that the demolition of historic buildings will be not acceptable in Smithfield," said Rogers.

9 Writing

Follow the instructions to write a paragraph about your vision for the future of your city. Use the Writing Checklist to check your work.

Think about your vision for the future of your city. How will your city have changed in fifty years? Will your city be larger or smaller? Will more people be living in the downtown area or in newer neighborhoods? What will have improved in fifty years? Will the crime be lower or higher? Why? Why do you think these changes will take place? On a separate sheet of paper, use your notes to write a paragraph describing the future of your city. Use future forms as appropriate.

Our city has had a lot of problems in the past, but I think it is going to be much better in 50 years. More companies are going to have offices in the downtown area, so people will be moving there to live closer to work. People will have fixed up the historic buildings downtown . . .

Writing Checklist

Reflect on your ability to use future forms by answering the questions.

☐ 1. Did you use future forms to make predictions or describe plans?

☐ 2. Did you use the future perfect to show a time relationship between two future situations?

☐ 3. Did you use any continuous forms to emphasize that a future activity is ongoing?

☐ 4. Did you use future forms with past and present forms?

☐ 5. Did you use time signals to clarify shifts in time?

☐ 6. Did you check your verb phrases for correct form?

Chapters 1–3

A. Choose the correct ending for each sentence.

1. I saw a traffic accident as _____.
   a. I have been driving to work
   b. I'm driving to work
   c. I was driving to work
2. By the time the chief executive arrives, _____.
   a. we'll have finished the project
   b. we finish the project
   c. we finished the project
3. Watch out! You _____.
   a. fall off the ladder
   b. will be falling off the ladder
   c. are going to fall off the ladder
4. My bus was late so when I got to school, the lecture _____.
   a. already started
   b. had already started
   c. has already started
5. How long have you and Cathy _____?
   a. know each other
   b. knew each other
   c. known each other
6. The education council never _____.
   a. meets on the first of the month
   b. is meeting on the first of the month
   c. been meeting on the first of the month
7. Someday, there _____.
   a. was no hunger in the world
   b. will be no hunger in the world
   c. isn't hunger in the world
8. My grandfather died before I was born, so _____.
   a. I have never met him
   b. I hadn't met him
   c. I never met him
9. On Earth, water _____.
   a. is boiling at 212 degrees Fahrenheit
   b. boils at 212 degrees Fahrenheit
   c. is going to boil at 212 degrees Fahrenheit
10. Ever since he was a child, Siridej _____.
    a. has wanted to see the Grand Canyon
    b. wants to see the Grand Canyon
    c. wanting to see the Grand Canyon
11. My ring was lost for three days. I can't believe _____.
    a. I've been finding it
    b. I've found it
    c. I was finding it
12. It's a well known fact that dolphins _____.
    a. are communicating by echolocation
    b. were communicating by echolocation
    c. communicate by echolocation
13. This time next week _____.
    a. they'll be taking the exam
    b. they're taking the exam
    c. they've taken the exam
14. When the movie began, it was a cold winter's night and the snow _____.
    a. fell
    b. was falling
    c. used to fall

B. Write the correct form of the verb in parentheses. More than one form may be correct.

15. I _____ (visit) friends in Washington on Saturday. I've booked the ticket.

16. No one knew how the rumor _____ (start) but it had spread throughout the office.

17. Most people _____ (not/understand) a word Professor Jakes says.

18. While you _____ (work), I've been relaxing at home.

19. Unfortunately, Rafik _____ (not/pay) last month's rent so his landlord is trying to evict him.

20. What on earth _____ you _____ (do)? You're soaking wet!

21. The principal _____ (announce) the test results tomorrow at noon.

22. The plane takes off at 7:20 and _____ (land) at 9:15.

23. Ted _____ (help) us. He's great with computers.

24. How long _____ she _____ (know) about the problem?

25. Sorry. You _____ (try) to say something when I interrupted you.

C. Find and correct the error in form, meaning, or use in each of these sentences.

26. How old are you in 2035?

_____

27. You say you love me but I'm not believing you.

_____

28. We're winning the game tomorrow.

_____

29. I didn't smoke a cigarette since last March.

_____

30. Please finish the report before you're going home tonight.

_____

4 Modals

FORM, MEANING, AND USE

 Examining Form

Read this article and complete the tasks below.

> ## Astrology and Psychology
>
> Many professionals in the field of psychology believe that astrology is outdated and irrelevant in today's world. They say people (shouldn't follow) the advice they read in their horoscopes. These professionals say that people must use astrology as a form of entertainment only. They fear that patients might take astrology too seriously and make bad decisions.
>
> Clinical psychologist Gary L. Burke, PhD, disagrees with these professionals, however. Dr. Burke says astrology is an ancient science that should be included in the practice of modern psychology. While he agrees that patients must not rely on astrology alone, he believes professional interpretation of a patient's astrological chart at birth may help the patient and psychologist gain a better understanding of a patient's thought process.
>
> Dr. Burke admits that there are many fraudulent astrology websites and businesses that offer people vague and useless information. He says patients shouldn't always follow the advice they read in a newspaper horoscope. "Many people make claims to be astrologists when they are really just writers looking to make some easy money. The public should not associate these people with the real science of professional astrology. There are many professional astrologists who offer high quality in-depth readings, however. We could combine their work with modern psychology to offer the best possible service to the modern public," says Dr. Burke.

irrelevant: not relating to the matter at hand; inapplicable
fraudulent: dishonest; not authentic

1. Circle eight examples of modals in the article.

2. Decide whether the following statements are true or false. Write *T* if the statement is true, *F* if it is false

   _____ a. All of the modals in this article are used in a present or future context.

   _____ b. This article contains at least one example of a modal showing lack of necessity.

2 Modals of Advice, Necessity, Prohibition, and Obligation

A. Read these sentences and complete the tasks below.

1. We had to finish dinner by 7:00 P.M.
2. You'd better spend more time studying so you can get good grades.
3. You don't have to finish all the work today.
4. I'm supposed to help Angie with her assignment.
5. He wasn't supposed to tell her the correct answers, but he did.
6. You should get another job if you need more money.
7. According to my lease, I couldn't keep a pet in my apartment.
8. We didn't have to buy any books for that class.
9. Students may not use their cell phones in class.
10. Everyone must arrive on time for the exam.

B. Complete the following tasks based on the sentences above.

1. Find two examples of advice: __2,__
   a. Which one is weaker? _____
   b. Which one is stronger? _____
2. Find two examples of necessity: _____
   a. Which one expresses a present/future context? _____
   b. Which one expresses a past context? _____
3. Find two examples of prohibition: _____
   a. Which one expresses a present/future context? _____
   b. Which one expresses a past context? _____
4. Find two examples of lack of necessity: _____
   a. Which one expresses a present/future context? _____
   b. Which one expresses a past context? _____
5. Find two examples of obligation: _____
   a. Which one expresses a present/future context? _____
   b. Which one expresses a past context? _____

3 Expressing Advice, Necessity and Obligation

Read the stories and write your advice for each one. Use as many modal forms as possible.

> When John woke up this morning, he felt very sick. He was going to stay home from work, but decided not to after he read his horoscope in the newspaper. His horoscope said: "Today is your day. Get out into the world! Just for today, you should tell everyone exactly what you are thinking. You will get amazing results!" First, John told his wife that she was a bad cook and she got very angry with him. When he went to work, he told his boss that she wasn't good at her job. Then John's best friend called to ask him for help with a project, but John said he didn't feel like helping. By the end of the day, John had lost his job and made many people angry!

1. _John should have stayed home from work._____
2. _____
3. _____
4. _____

Katya was visiting friends for the first time in several years. Her friends were overjoyed to see her and prepared a big meal to celebrate her arrival. The main part of the meal was shrimp, which Katya is allergic to. Katya didn't want to appear rude in front of her friends, so she ate a large plateful. About an hour later, Katya became ill and had to excuse herself. Her friends didn't know about the allergy, so they didn't understand why she had left the table. They were upset.

1. Katya _____

2. _____

3. _____

4. _____

4 Understanding Modals of Possibility

Choose the correct response to each statement or question. There may be more than one correct answer for each.

1. "Heather hasn't called today. She might be busy at work." The speaker . . .
   a. is sure that Heather is busy.
   b. isn't sure whether Heather is busy.
   c. does not know for sure why Heather has not called.
   d. isn't sure whether Heather called or not.

2. "Has Scott left already? He couldn't have finished all the homework so quickly." The speaker . . .
   a. is absolutely certain that Scott hasn't finished his homework.
   b. isn't sure whether Scott has finished his homework.
   c. believes that Scott studies too much.
   d. is surprised that Scott is no longer studying.

3. "I saw the doctor last week, so I should get the test results today." The speaker is . . .
   a. positive he will get the test results today.
   b. making an assumption.
   c. fairly certain he will get the test results today.
   d. certain he will not get the test results today.

4. "Carolina didn't eat anything at lunch. She might have eaten before she arrived." The speaker . . .
   a. is sure that Carolina ate before lunch.
   b. is making a guess about why Carolina didn't eat at lunch.
   c. is not sure whether Carolina ate at lunch.
   d. has a lot of proof that Carolina ate before lunch.

5. "Al called three times today. He must have something urgent to discuss." The speaker is . . .
   a. fairly certain that Al has something urgent to discuss.
   b. drawing a conclusion about why Al called three times in one day.
   c. not sure how many times Al called.
   d. not sure whether Al wants to talk to her.

6. "The concert ought to have ended by now. It's already 10:00." The speaker . . .
   a. is positive that the concert has ended.
   b. knows exactly when the concert will end.
   c. is not positive that the concert has ended.
   d. is making an assumption.

7. "I bought my mom new gloves but I'm afraid she may not like them. The speaker . . .
   a. has already shown the gloves to her mom.
   b. is certain that her mom will not like the gloves.
   c. is certain that her mom will like the gloves.
   d. does not know whether her mom will like the gloves.

8. "My boss just gave me a promotion! I couldn't be happier." The speaker . . .
   a. believes it would be impossible to be any happier right now.
   b. is very happy.
   c. does not want the promotion.
   d. is not certain how she feels.

5 Contrasting Modal Forms

Choose the best modal to complete each sentence.

1. I (couldn't have/shouldn't have) eaten all that chocolate. Now I feel sick!

2. Horoscopes (may be/must be) entertaining, but they're not factual.

3. All employees (must/could) arrive by 7:30 in order to open the store at 8:00.

4. Erin isn't here yet. She (might have/should have) forgotten our date.

5. You (don't have to/may not) leave early. It's against the rules.

6. You (might/had better) study tonight or you will fail the test.

7. We (ought to/were supposed to) hurry. Class starts in three minutes!

8. Akiko (doesn't have to/must not) work tomorrow. It's a holiday.

9. They (couldn't/shouldn't) see the exhibit because the museum was closed.

10. Corey (is supposed to/might not) arrive on time. He's always late!

6 Completing Conversations with Modals

Complete this conversation using the correct form of the words in parentheses. Use contractions when possible.

Shawn: It's strange. Christina _was supposed to work_ (be supposed to/work) on the project with me on
                                                    1
           Friday, but she didn't show up.

Lori: Really? That's unusual for her. She _____ (must/not/remember). She _____
                                                              2
          (might/be) really busy yesterday. I hope that's why she wasn't there. Do you think something bad
           3
          _____ (may/happen) to her?
                   4

Shawn: I hope not! I suppose she could be upset with me for some reason. I was teasing her about something

           last week and I guess she might have taken it the wrong way.

Lori: I doubt that's why she didn't show up. She has a great sense of humor. No, wait a minute – she

          _____ (not/have to/work) on Friday afternoons, does she?
                   5

Shawn: You're right, but I think she _____ (be supposed/to work) last Friday because the project
                                                                6
           manager was out sick. Do you think I _____ (should/ask) her why she didn't show up next
                                                           7
           time I see her?

Lori: Yes, why not? I'm sure there _____ (must/be) an explanation for it.
                                              8

Find and correct the errors. The first one has been corrected for you.

HOROSCOPE

ARIES (March 21–April 20) You should ~~been~~ *be* walking on air right now! The stars are in line and you just may getting everything your heart desires this month.

TAURUS (April 21–May 20) Wake up! You should to be out socializing more. You have been unhappy, but your social life could be more exciting this month.

GEMINI (May 21–June 20) You had not better spend all your money this month. Mars is urging you to splurge, so you must be careful to make good decisions.

CANCER (June 21–July 21) You could have problems with your partner this month. Work hard to keep the peace even when your sweetie is being less than sweet.

LEO (July 22–August 21) You couldn't be happier! You should have great luck in love and at work this month. You may even get that proposal you've wanted.

VIRGO (August 22–September 21) Don't look now, but you could be in trouble. You should have been so careless last month.

LIBRA (September 22–October 21) This month should be life-changing for you. You will finally be excited about that big change on the horizon.

SCORPIO (October 22–November 21) You could has worked harder last month. Now you must working hard to make up for all the fun you had then!

SAGITTARIUS (November 22–December 20) You'd better not made any big decisions this month. Venus is in the area to cause problems and confusion.

CAPRICORN (December 21–January 19) You don't has to solve that problem this month, but you will feel a lot better if you do. You may even get more money.

AQUARIUS (January 20–February 18) You might not seeing great results this month, but everything you do should lead to prosperity in the future.

PISCES (February 19–March 20) You should see big changes at work this month. You may wanted to be on the lookout for a big announcement.

Follow the instructions to write two paragraphs about a time when you made a mistake. Use modals to explain the mistake. Use adverbs of time if necessary for clarification. Then use the Writing Checklist to check your work.

In the first paragraph, write the mistake you made. Under which circumstances did you make the mistake? How did the mistake affect your life? In the second paragraph, write about ways to avoid such a mistake. What could you have done differently? How could you have avoided the mistake? Who could have helped you? What can you do differently to avoid such a mistake in the future?

I was supposed to give a presentation to the marketing department at work last week. Everyone was gathered in the conference room, but I couldn't remember the name of the marketing manager. I had to introduce her to my co-worker, and I accidentally called her by the wrong name.

Writing Checklist

Reflect on your ability to use modals by answering the questions.

☐ 1. Did you use modals to explain possible situations or make guesses?

☐ 2. Did you use modals to draw conclusions?

☐ 3. Did you use modals to give advice or suggest a possible course of action?

☐ 4. Did you use modals to make predictions about a future situation?

☐ 5. Did you use adverbs with or in place of modals?

☐ 6. Did you check your verb phrases for correct form?

5 The Passive

FORM, MEANING, AND USE

 Examining Form

Read this article and complete the tasks below.

COLLEGE ENTRANCE EXAMS

Every year, millions of students apply to enter colleges and universities in the United States. Many of these students are required to take standardized college entrance exams. Their exam scores can be sent directly to the colleges of their choice. The exams are very difficult and last for many hours. The students must pay a fee and arrive at the testing site early in the morning. Some of the exams test general aptitude, while others test subjects that students are expected to learn in high school, including mathematics, science, and English. The questions are chosen by a group of educators and researchers.

Colleges and universities use the exam scores, along with an applicant's high school grades to determine whether the applicant will be admitted. A college or university may also consider a student's extracurricular activities and work history when making decisions about admission.

Some people feel that colleges and universities pay too much attention to these exam scores. They feel other factors, such as high school grades and extracurricular activities, should be considered more carefully. Other people believe the tests are a fair and accurate way to predict how successful the student will be in college. They say high school grades are assigned differently by each teacher, but standardized tests are the same for everyone. No matter what people say about standardized college entrance exams, they are likely to be used in the United States for many years to come.

standardized: the same everywhere
applicant: a person who is applying for something
extracurricular: outside of class, not required

1. Circle six examples of the passive.
2. Choose two of the passive sentences you circled and change them to active sentences.

_____

_____

2 Contrasting Passive Forms

Choose one, two, or three correct phrases to complete each statement or question.

1. The test _____ orally tomorrow.
   a. was given   b. will be given   c. should be given

2. The homework _____ very quickly.
   a. was completed   b. will be completed   c. must be completed

3. The teacher's question _____ by another student before I could raise my hand.
   a. is answered   b. had been answered   c. could be answered

4. One hundred new applications _____ by our university every day.
   a. were reviewed   b. must be reviewed   c. are reviewed

5. The instructions _____ aloud when John arrived.
   a. are read   b. are going to be read   c. were being read

6. The testing website _____ by 4,300 students last week.
   a. was viewed   b. is viewed   c. should be viewed

3 Practicing Active and Passive Sentences

Six university students live together in a house near campus. On Saturday, they all worked together to clean the house. The chart shows which roommate completed each chore.

CHORE	ROOMMATE
Wash the dishes	Kenzie
Sweep the floor	Ashley
Clean the bathroom	Heather
Wash the clothes	Jasette
Iron the clothes	Akiko
Take out the trash	Danielle

A. Use the chart to complete the sentences with active or passive forms.

1. The dishes _were washed by Kenzie._____
2. Akiko _____
3. The floor _____
4. The trash _____
5. The bathroom _____
6. Jasette _____

B. Choose three of your answers and change them to active sentences.

1. _Kenzie washed the dishes._____
2. _____
3. _____
4. _____

28   Chapter 5

4 Identifying the Agent in Passive Sentences

Read the passive sentences below and circle the agent in each sentence.

1. Last year, this exam was taken by (two million students.)
2. Our class was taught by a graduate teaching assistant.
3. The cars were entirely assembled by high-tech machines.
4. The frogs will be dissected by the anatomy students.
5. The school was damaged by hurricane-force winds.
6. The museum exhibit was viewed by three hundred thousand visitors.

5 Thinking About the Omitted Agent

The agent is omitted in each of the following sentences. Read each sentence and then place a check mark next to the reason the agent was omitted.

1. It is said that high cholesterol can cause heart disease.

   __✓__ a. The author is avoiding a general subject.   _____ b. The author is avoiding blame.

2. Many hamburgers are eaten in the school cafeteria.

   _____ a. The agent is obvious.   _____ b. The agent is unknown.

3. All of the exams have been corrected.

   _____ a. The author is avoiding a general subject.   _____ b. The agent is unimportant.

4. My car was damaged in the parking lot while I was in class.

   _____ a. The author is avoiding a general subject.   _____ b. The agent is unknown.

5. College entrance exams have been overused in America.

   _____ a. The agent is obvious.   _____ b. The author is avoiding a general subject.

6. Art therapy can be used to complement traditional psychotherapy.

   _____ a. The agent is obvious.   _____ b. The author is avoiding a general subject.

6 Changing Active Sentences to Passive Sentences

Change these active sentences to passive sentences where possible. Omit the agent if you think it is unnecessary. If a sentence cannot be changed, write an *X* on the line.

1. Someone vandalized the school last night.
   The school was vandalized last night.

2. Your children broke my window!
   _____

3. These students will become excellent doctors.
   _____

4. People eat a lot of rice in Japan.
   _____

5. They're going to hold a fund-raising event next week.
   _____

6. English teachers should teach proper grammar in high school.
   _____

7. Every student should take the exam preparation course.
   _____

8. These textbooks cost $150 each!

_____

9. The policeman stopped the traffic at the intersection.

_____

10. A guest speaker is giving the lecture.

_____

11. The United States is the fifth largest Spanish-speaking country.

_____

12. Someone stole my husband's wallet yesterday.

_____

7 Contrasting Active Sentences and Passive Sentences

Complete this paragraph by circling the best form of the verbs in parentheses.

Reporter: This is Morris Franklin coming to you live from downtown Springfield. I'm on the scene of a very
serious accident. Earlier this evening, two cars (were collided/collided) in this intersection. As you can see, the
1
cars (were damaged/damaged) very badly, but it is unclear whether anyone (was hurt/hurt). Right now, many
2   3
bystanders (are being gathered/are gathering) at the scene. We (are being told/are telling) by the authorities that
4   5
this accident may (have been caused/have caused) by a broken traffic signal. Rebecca Goldberg (was seen/saw)
6   7
the accident happen. Let's talk with Rebecca now . . .

8 Editing

Find and correct the errors. The first one has been corrected for you.

Morris: Good evening, Rebecca. Thank you for taking time to speak with us. I want you to know that this
_is_
interview ~~are~~ being seen by our viewers at home. Where were you when the accident occurred?

Rebecca: Good evening, Morris. I was standing right here on this corner. That yellow car is hit by the blue car as
it was going through the intersection.

Morris: Were anyone hurt?

Rebecca: Well, I'm no doctor, but I'd say the driver of the blue car was injure pretty badly.

Morris: How do you know that?

Rebecca: Well, as he was be pulled out of the car by the paramedics, he was yelling about his right arm. One of
the paramedics said it may have been broke.

Morris: And what about the passengers and the driver of the yellow car?

Rebecca: I didn't see any passengers. The driver of the yellow car were taken to the hospital as a precaution, but
he told the paramedics that he felt fine.

Morris: Well, that's good news. Were you hit by any flying debris from the crash?

Rebecca: No, I weren't.

Follow the instructions to write two paragraphs about a problem in modern education. Pay attention to shifts in focus and choose active or passive verbs that improve the flow of ideas. Then use the Writing Checklist to check your work.

> In the first paragraph, write about a problem in education. What is the problem? Why does it occur? Who does it affect? Why is it important? In the second paragraph, write about your suggestions for improving the situation. Who can help solve this problem? What must be done in order to improve the situation? How can these changes be implemented?

In the United States, it is believed that everyone should be able to go to go the college. However, higher education is very expensive. Sometimes it is very difficult for students to buy textbooks and other necessary materials. These books are sold in bookstores for ridiculously high prices. One textbook may cost several hundred dollars. Even the used textbooks are very expensive. Used textbooks are sold online, but they have often been ruined by the previous owner . . .

Writing Checklist

Reflect on your ability to use the passive by answering the questions.

☐ 1. Did you use the passive to state a general truth or idea?
☐ 2. Did you use the passive to talk about a process?
☐ 3. Did you use the passive to keep the focus on a single subject?
☐ 4. Did you use the passive to help keep the focus when changing subjects?
☐ 5. Did you avoid overusing the passive?
☐ 6. Did you check your sentences for correct verb phrases?

6 Nouns and Noun Modifiers

FORM, MEANING, AND USE

1 Examining Form

Read this student essay and complete the tasks below.

My Visit to Costa Rica

My best friend had to go to (Costa Rica) for business this summer. After studying some tourist <u>information</u>, I decided to go with her and spend some extra time touring the country. Costa Rica is not very far from the United States, but we had to take three separate flights to get to our first destination, Playa Samara. Playa Samara is a small beach town located in the Guanacaste peninsula. It has one of the most beautiful beaches in the world, and the town is rustic and friendly. We stayed in a tiny inn right on the beach. The water was magnificent and we enjoyed at least an hour of swimming every day.

After leaving Playa Samara, we toured many other famous areas in the country, including the Arenal Volcano, the Monteverde Cloud Forest, and the Tortuguero area on the Caribbean coast. I had never been outside the United States before and I was really excited to see what life is like in Central America. The weather was very hot near the beach, but it was much cooler in the center of the country, where the elevation is higher. Summer is the rainy season in Costa Rica, so there was a rain shower almost every afternoon. The food was wonderful. We ate rice and chicken every day and almost always had a piece of tropical fruit with our breakfast. In San Jose, the capital, I did a lot of shopping while my friend researched business opportunities. She owns a business called Exotic Furniture that imports furniture to the United States, and she made some business contacts in Costa Rica. I hope she works with them often, because I want to visit the country again soon.

---

1. Circle five proper nouns in the article.

2. Underline five noncount nouns in the article.

2 Thinking About Meaning and Use

Read each sentence and the statements that follow. Choose the correct statement by thinking about the meaning and use of the underlined words. There may be more than one correct answer for each.

1. Drinking <u>water</u> is very healthy.
   a. This sentence is about a specific serving of water.
   b. This sentence is about water in general.
   c. *Water* is plural.

2. Joe caught a <u>fish</u> yesterday and his brother caught three <u>fish</u>.
   a. The first noun refers to one item; the second refers to more than one.
   b. Both nouns refer to one item.
   c. Both nouns refer to fish in general.

3. The success <u>of the business</u> encouraged other companies to invest here.
   a. The sentence talks about success in general.
   b. The sentence talks about a particular type of success.
   c. The underlined word modify success.

4. The <u>audience</u> is applauding loudly.
   a. The sentence is about a group of people.
   b. They are clapping their hands, according to the sentence.
   c. *Audience* has a plural form.

5. He was a <u>mean, demanding</u> boss.
   a. *Mean* describes a quality of the boss.
   b. *Demanding* describes a quality of the boss.
   c. *Mean* and *demanding* form a compound adjective.

6. I really like <u>candy</u>, but eating ten pieces of <u>candy</u> made me feel sick.
   a. Both nouns refer to candy in general.
   b. The first noun's quantity is known, but the second cannot be counted.
   c. The second noun's quantity is known, but the first cannot be counted.

7. My boss often goes <u>scuba diving</u> in Belize.
   a. *Scuba diving* is a compound noun.
   b. *Scuba diving* has a plural form.
   c. *Scuba* describes *diving*.

8. The <u>economy</u> in <u>Costa Rica</u> is growing rapidly.
   a. The first noun is a common noun; the second one is a proper noun.
   b. The second noun is a common noun; the first one is a proper noun.
   c. Both nouns are common nouns.

3 Using Adjective Modifiers

Rearrange the words in parentheses to write an answer for each question.

1. **Q:** What did you buy Beth for her birthday?
   A: (bought/her/a/I/big/blanket/fleece/nice) *I bought her a nice big fleece blanket.*

2. **Q:** What did they see at the museum?
   A: (ancient/saw/some/They/pottery/Roman) _____

3. **Q:** What did you buy at the store?
   A: (bought/a/reading/small/I/lamp/black) _____

4. **Q:** Where was the meeting held?
   A: (It/beautiful/was/in a/theater/old) _____

5. **Q:** Which of those women is Lindsey?
   A: (pink/is/wearing the/brown/Lindsey/and/sweater) _____

6. **Q:** What do you want for your office?
   A: (wooden/I/table/want/a/rectangular) _____

4 Using Compound Modifiers

Combine the words in the box to create a compound modifier for each sentence below.

1. We loved the _____-_____ cherries because they were so sweet.

2. It's only a _____-_____ drive from my house to work.

3. He's a very _____-_____ man. He isn't nice to anyone.

4. It's really a _____-_____ show. It's been playing on Broadway for ten years.

5. It's illegal to buy _____-_____ cigars in the United States.

6. Eating too many _____-_____ foods can make you gain weight.

long	calorie
chocolate	spirited
high	mile
Cuban	running
mean	made
five	covered

5 Understanding Nouns with Count and Noncount Meaning

Read the sentences below. Write *C* if the underlined noun is used with count meaning. Write *N* if the underlined noun is used with noncount meaning.

__C__ 1. We signed all the underline{papers} and received the check.

_____ 2. I never drink soda.

_____ 3. Education can be very expensive

_____ 4. They caught the woman who committed the crime.

_____ 5. I used a mild detergent to clean the floor.

_____ 6. Chocolate is my weakness!

_____ 7. This room needs more light.

_____ 8. We cooked the whole chicken.

6 Understanding Subject-Verb Agreement With Nouns

Complete the sentences below by circling the appropriate verb form in parentheses.

1. The students (is learning/are learning) about Central America.

2. The jury (is deciding/are deciding) the verdict now.

3. *A Farewell to Arms* (is/are) a novel by Ernest Hemingway.

4. This stack of papers (is/are) ready to be graded.

5. Five deer (was playing/were playing) in the forest while we were walking.

6. The United States (has/have) many Spanish-speaking residents.

7. My company assets (is being invested/are being invested) in Costa Rica.

8. Buddhism (is/are) a popular world religion.

9. The box of software (belongs/belong) to tech support.

10. Crime (is/are) on the rise in that city.

11. The five-mile race (was/were) difficult for me.

12. The girl with the red hair (wants/want) an appointment.

13. Two teaspoons of oil (is required/are required) to make the brownies.

14. Abby's interest in insects (seems/seem) genuine.

7 Using Prepositional Phrases

A. Use the correct preposition from the box to complete each sentence. Use some prepositions more than once.

1. We need three cups __of__ sugar for this recipe.
2. I'm working on a degree _____ international business.
3. The fight caused a lot of damage _____ their relationship.
4. The texture _____ the fabric was unusual.
5. We are hoping to have more scholarships _____ our students this year.
6. The flight _____ San Jose has been delayed.
7. I can't remember the name _____ the book.
8. I donated a pint _____ blood today.
9. The success _____ the company has been remarkable.
10. Ashley needed help _____ her homework.

of	to
in	with
for	

B. Three of the prepositional phrases created in part A show possession. Write the number of these sentences on the line below.

_____

8 Using Compound Nouns

Complete these paragraphs by filling in the compound nouns described in parentheses.

A. Yesterday I went to the _____bookstore_____ (store that sells books) to look for information
1
about business in Central America. I found a great one about the _____ (a hobby
2
in which people go diving underwater using SCUBA tanks) industry. This is especially popular on

the Caribbean coast where there is a large _____ (reef made of coral). I paid for
3

the book with my _____ (card that is used for credit) and walked out of the store
4

through the _____ (door that is used as an exit).
5

B. I really love my new home. It has all the modern amenities. We have a very efficient

_____ (machine that washes dishes) in the kitchen and a _____
1   2
(machine that washes clothes) in the utility room. We even have a new _____
3
(machine that dries clothes). I recently bought some _____ (lamps that stand on
4

the floor) and some _____ (lamps that sit on a table) for the living room. The
5

guest bedroom is very comfortable, so I hope we have some _____ (guests that
6
stay in the house) soon.

Find and correct the errors. The first one has been corrected for you.

Let's Get With the Times

I am responding to the opinion column written by Frank in Newtonville. My opinion and his opinion ~~is~~ *are*

very different. Frank doesn't believe that American-own companies should have any involvement

to international firms. Frank is afraid there will be many problems with the economy if we invest in

Central American countries. Well, there is many problems with the economy right now, and we are

solving it by investing in Central American countries. I belong to a three-years-old international

business group. Our group are working every day to improve the economy in the United States

and other countries. Researches shows that by working together, we can achieve great results.

Cooperation and understanding is our greatest tools at this time.

Follow the instructions to write a descriptive paragraph. Use the Writing Checklist to check your work.

Think about your hometown. What is it like? List some interesting qualities of the town. Then write notes describing people and places in the town. On a separate sheet of paper, use your notes to write a detailed paragraph describing your hometown. Be sure to explain how you feel about your hometown. Then use the Writing Checklist to check your work.

My hometown is a very small place. It doesn't seem to have a lot of special qualities at first, but it's a really great place to live. The people in the town are very friendly. Your neighbor will give you a cup of sugar anytime you need it, for example. Many townspeople volunteer after school to help the local students with their studies. There is a craft guild that meets at Kepler Auditorium every Wednesday evening . . .

Writing Checklist

Reflect on your ability to use nouns by answering the questions.

- ☐ 1. Did you capitalize all proper nouns?
- ☐ 2. Did you check for subject-verb agreement with nouns?
- ☐ 3. Did you use plurals correctly with compound nouns and modifiers?
- ☐ 4. Did you use synonyms and pronouns to avoid repetition?
- ☐ 5. Did you use pronouns and antecedents clearly?
- ☐ 6. Did you add details to your writing?

Chapters 4–6

A. Rewrite these sentences. Do not change the meaning. Use the modals in the box. Change the form as necessary.

don't have to	can't	ought to	have got to	couldn't
be supposed to	could	may not	should	must

1. All employees are required to attend the annual general meeting.

   _____

2. It would have been a good idea if you'd seen a doctor about your headaches.

   _____

3. It's imperative that you quit smoking.

   _____

4. It wasn't necessary for you to buy me flowers.

   _____

5. Everyone is expected to complete the assignment.

   _____

6. He should have told me that he was allergic to peanuts!

   _____

7. You weren't allowed to use cell phones in the hospital so I went outside.

   _____

8. Maybe it won't snow tomorrow.

   _____

9. It's impossible that Steph is out. I just spoke with her!

   _____

10. There's a possibility that you're right this time.

    _____

B. Find the incorrect sentences and correct them. If a sentence is correct, put a check (✓).

_____ 11. A question was asked the professor.

_____ 12. I'm not suited by this color.

_____ 13. Many languages are spoken in New York.

_____ 14. The college library is be cleaned tomorrow so we can't use it.

_____ 15. The project is being completed by two freelance engineers.

_____ 16. I've already told you I'm agreed with you.

_____ 17. It is thought that dinosaurs were wiped out by a meteorite.

_____ 18. My apartment locates downtown.

_____ 19. The contract must be signed before we can proceed.

_____ 20. Has been sent the confirmation letter yet?

C. Six of these ideas can be rewritten as compound nouns. Which ones? Rewrite them.

21. a schedule of buses

_____

22. the paws of a cat

_____

23. a book about geography

_____

24. soup made from chicken

_____

25. a movie about a child

_____

26. a store that sells books

_____

27. food that is junk

_____

28. food that is tasty

_____

29. flakes made of corn

_____

30. a song about flowers

_____

D. Put the modifiers into the correct order.

31. a rabbit: short-eared, small

_____

32. boots: hiking, leather

_____

33. a movie: black-and-white, old

_____

34. a vase: delicate, Chinese

_____

35. sculpture: metal, large

_____

7 Articles and Other Determiners

FORM, MEANING, AND USE

1 Examining Form

Read the following article from a university newspaper and complete the tasks below.

> ## Meet Professor Busseni
>
> Some of you have already met Professor Chiara Busseni, a visiting professor of art history. She arrived in New York City in August and will be teaching at our university for two years. She comes from Italy and is an expert in Renaissance sculpture. I recently had a chance meet Professor Busseni and hear her impressions of life in our city. "New York City is so alive and vibrant," she said. "There is so much diversity in <u>the city</u>, which is exciting. <u>It</u> can seem big and overwhelming at first, but I already feel at home here." Professor Busseni said every Sunday she enjoys eating a traditional American breakfast at a diner near her apartment. She sometimes visits the Little Italy neighborhood when she wants to hear her native language or buy Italian items. Most of the time, though, she chooses to try new things. She loves New York City's wide variety of foods and other goods from around the world. She also relishes visiting a different museum every weekend, such as the Guggenheim.
>
> When I asked Professor Busseni to tell me her favorite place in the city, she enthusiastically said, "Oh, Central Park is the best! I love going to the park on a warm afternoon when I can eat an ice cream cone and read. I even grade my students' papers there. It's a very relaxing place." So what is her least favorite part of the city? "The traffic!" she says. "But I'm getting used to it." It seems as though New York City has made a great impression on Professor Busseni. Let's give her a warm welcome to our university.

Renaissance: a period of great artistic and scientific achievement in the 15th and 16th centuries in Europe
impressions: observations and opinions
vibrant: lively, full of energy

overwhelming: crushing, overpowering
relishes: enjoys greatly

1. Look at the circled and underlined words in the reading. They show an example of previously mentioned information being simplified when it is referred to again. Find a similar set of nouns and pronouns in the reading and underline each word.

2. Find examples of the following things: _____
   a. A definite article used with a proper noun: _____
   b. A possessive adjective: _____
   c. An indefinite article used with a nonspecific noun: _____
   d. A definite article used with a familiar or unique noun: _____

Read each sentence and the statements that follow. Check (✓) the correct statement or statements for each. There may be more than one correct statement.

1. Let's go out to a nice restaurant for dinner.

    _____ a. The speaker has a specific restaurant in mind.

    _____ b. The listener has a specific restaurant in mind.

    __✓__ c. The speaker doesn't have a specific restaurant in mind.

2. Grizzly bears are native to Alaska.

    _____ a. This sentence identifies a specific bear.

    _____ b. The subject of this sentence is a generic noun.

    _____ c. The listener has a specific grizzly bear in mind.

3. Raj went to a book club meeting yesterday and really enjoyed it. He'll probably attend the meeting again next month.

    _____ a. The speaker has a specific meeting in mind.

    _____ b. Both sentences refer to the same meeting.

    _____ c. Neither the speaker nor the listener has a specific meeting in mind.

4. Do you want to go to the mall after work?

    _____ a. The speaker has a specific mall in mind.

    _____ b. The listener has a specific mall in mind.

    _____ c. "Mall" is a familiar noun.

5. I saw a very interesting play last night.

    _____ a. The speaker has a specific play in mind.

    _____ b. The listener has a specific play in mind.

    _____ c. "Play" is a unique noun.

6. Please don't leave your keys on the counter anymore.

    _____ a. The speaker has a specific set of keys in mind.

    _____ c. The speaker has a specific counter in mind.

    _____ d. The listener has a specific counter in mind.

3 **Contrasting Articles**

Complete these paragraphs with *a/an, the,* or no article (Ø).

A. Everywhere you look in our city, there are major problems. _____the_____ ground is covered
   ₁

   in _____ litter, and _____ subway is filthy. _____ crime is on
           2   3   4

   the rise here, as well. If we don't do anything, _____ city will be unlivable within three
                                                            5

   years. I think we can make _____ change for the better, however. If _____
                                        6   7

   residents of each neighborhood are willing to meet and discuss ways to improve their neighborhood,

   _____ progress will be made. If you agree with me, why not organize _____
          8   9

   meeting in your neighborhood today?

B. I love visiting _____ zoo. I just saw _____ advertisement saying that there will
                          1   2

   be _____ gorillas there for the first time in five years. I can't wait to see _____
              3   4

gorillas because I read _____ interesting article about _____ primates
$\quad\quad\quad\quad\quad\quad\quad\quad\quad\quad$ 5 $\quad\quad\quad\quad\quad\quad\quad\quad\quad\quad$ 6

recently. Did you know that _____ gorilla is even capable of learning sign language?
$\quad\quad\quad\quad\quad\quad\quad\quad\quad\quad\quad\quad$ 7

4 Using Demonstrative Adjectives to Identify Specific Nouns

Complete these paragraphs with *this*, *that*, *these*, or *those*.

A. ____This____ city is my home and I love it. I plan to live here for the rest of my life, but
$\quad\quad\quad$ 1

I still have happy memories of 1998. _____ year, I lived in Chicago. Although
$\quad\quad\quad\quad\quad\quad\quad\quad\quad\quad\quad\quad\quad\quad\quad$ 2

_____ city was too large for me, there are a lot of things about it that I miss. I remember
$\quad\quad$ 3

all _____ stores on Michigan Avenue and how much fun it was to go shopping there.
$\quad\quad\quad$ 4

Maybe I will even take my family there on vacation _____ year.
$\quad\quad\quad\quad\quad\quad\quad\quad\quad\quad\quad\quad\quad\quad\quad\quad\quad\quad\quad\quad\quad$ 5

B. Right now I'm watching television coverage of New Year's Eve celebrations in Asia. _____
$\quad\quad\quad\quad\quad\quad\quad\quad\quad\quad\quad\quad\quad\quad\quad\quad\quad\quad\quad\quad\quad\quad\quad\quad\quad\quad\quad\quad\quad\quad\quad\quad\quad\quad\quad\quad$ 1

TV broadcast is doing a great job of showing all the parties and events. It seems like

_____ cities over there really have elaborate celebrations at _____ time of
$\quad\quad$ 2 $\quad\quad\quad\quad\quad\quad\quad\quad\quad\quad\quad\quad\quad\quad\quad\quad\quad\quad\quad$ 3

year. Tokyo looks especially interesting. I would love to go there in order to see all _____
$\quad\quad\quad\quad\quad\quad\quad\quad\quad\quad\quad\quad\quad\quad\quad\quad\quad\quad\quad\quad\quad\quad\quad\quad\quad\quad\quad\quad\quad\quad\quad\quad\quad\quad\quad\quad$ 4

fireworks. Oh, well. At least I can watch them on TV.

5 Contrasting Definite and Indefinite Articles

A. Read this conversation and complete the tasks.

Sheila: Hey, do you see that man over there? He's standing at the end of the line.

Lindsey: Do you mean the man wearing a red shirt? Yes. Why do you ask?

Sheila: He looks just like Beth's boyfriend, Bill.

Lindsey: No, that's not him. Bill is much taller.

Sheila: Oh, I guess you're right. Have you spoken with Beth lately? I haven't heard from
her all week and I'm starting to get worried about her. We usually talk every day.

Lindsey: Yes, I called her last night. She's been working nights writing a paper on semantics.

Sheila: Oh, that's right! She said she was going to work with a coworker every night this week.

Lindsey: Poor Beth! I don't know how she manages to stay awake for so long.

Sheila: She's probably at the library right now. Should we take her a cup of coffee on our way home?

Lindsey: That's a good idea. I'll bet she'd like that.

B. Read these sentences from the conversation and look at the underlined nouns. Match each sentence to its use.

1. Hey, do you see that <u>man</u> over there?

2. He's standing at the <u>end</u> of the line.

3. Do you mean the <u>man</u> wearing a red shirt?

4. . . . and also writing a paper on <u>semantics</u>.

5. She said she was going to work with a <u>coworker</u> this week.

6. She's probably at the <u>library</u> right now.

<u> 3 </u> **a.** The underlined noun can be easily identified by the listener.

_____ **b.** The underlined noun is generic.

_____ **c.** The underlined noun is not specific for speaker or the listener.

_____ **d.** The underlined noun is unique.

_____ **e.** The underlined noun is far from the speaker and the listener.

_____ **f.** The underlined noun is familiar.

6 **Responding to Questions**

Read the advertisement on the poster. Then answer the questions that follow using complete sentences. Check for proper use of articles and other determiners.

1. What is the poster advertising?

   _____

2. What time will the event begin?

   _____

3. What should you bring if you want to attend?

   _____

4. Where will the event take place?

   _____

5. What kind of musician will perform?

   _____

6. Why is the event taking place?

   _____

7. Have you ever attended a similar event?

   _____

8. Is there a homeless shelter in your city?

   _____

Who? ♪ Accomplished guitarist Ricky Johnson

What? Outdoor summertime concert

Where? Municipal Park Bandshell

When? Saturday, July 23 at 6:30 in the evening

Why? Fundraiser to benefit The City Shelter

Price? Donation of a nonperishable food item to help stock the shelter's pantry.

Please help us keep the shelter's services available for those in need. We hope to see everyone there!

7 **Working with Articles and Other Determiners**

Match each question with a logical response. Then add *a/an*, or *the* to each response.

1. Do you enjoy living in the city? <u> e </u>

2. What are you eating for dinner this evening? _____

3. Is there anything I need to do today? _____

4. Do you like the cookies I baked? _____

5. What should we do tonight? _____

6. Where is Bob? _____

a. Let's go see _____ movie.

b. He's in there talking to _____ president.

c. They're very good, but I prefer _____ ones you baked last week.

d. I'm going to cook _____ steak on the grill.

e. It's very exciting, but I prefer living out in <u>the</u> country.

f. Yes, you need to go to _____ bank after work.

Find and correct the errors. The first one has been corrected for you.

Living in~~a~~ big city has many advantages and disadvantages. It is sometimes difficult to get
around quickly because of a traffic. When walking down the crowded street, it's easy for a person
to lose the wallet to a pickpocket if he's not careful. There is also a lot of pollution in a big city.
On the other hand, there are many fun things to do in a city. In Chicago, for example, you can go
to the top of a Sears Tower. In Washington D.C. you can visit Smithsonian Institution. In Detroit
you can see the baseball game at Comerica Park. Then, after a game you can have dinner at the
Hard Rock Cafe. In New York City, you can eat a good food at a neighborhood deli. For me, the
advantages of living in a big city outweigh the disadvantages.

9 **Writing**

Follow the instructions to write a descriptive paragraph. Use the Writing Checklist to check your work.

Think carefully about your favorite season or time of year. Why is it your favorite time of year? What
activities happen at that time? Are there any holidays at that time? What do you see, smell, hear,
and taste at that time of year? Make some detailed notes of your observations and memories. On a
separate sheet of paper, use your notes to write a detailed paragraph describing your favorite season
or time of year. When you write, pay attention to the articles and other determiners you use to
introduce the nouns. When do you need a determiner?

Spring is my favorite time of year. I always look forward to the warm air and melting snow. The
air smells so nice in the spring, especially when the flowers begin blooming. I like to go to the
park in the spring so I can see all the beautiful gardens . . .

> **Writing Checklist**
>
> **Reflect on your ability to use articles by answering the questions.**
> ☐ 1. Did you use definite articles with specific nouns?
> ☐ 2. Did you use indefinite articles with non-specific nouns?
> ☐ 3. Did you use an article or determiner with all singular count nouns?
> ☐ 4. Did you use articles correctly with generic nouns?
> ☐ 5. Did you use definite articles with appropriate proper nouns?
> ☐ 6. Did you use the correct pronouns, possessive adjectives or nouns, and demonstratives
>   where appropriate?

8 Quantifiers

FORM, MEANING, AND USE

 Examining Form

Read this advertising leaflet and complete the tasks.

Why Choose SuperMegaTech?

(A lot of) people have been asking us why they should choose *SuperMegaTech* when a few cut-rate companies are offering communication services for about ten dollars less per month. That's an excellent question, and we have the answer for you: *SuperMegaTech* is simply the best value out there. We are equipped to take care of all of your personal communication needs. None of the other companies has a network as good as ours and our customer service can't be beat. We treat each customer like somebody special and almost all of our customers report that they are "very satisfied" with both our network and our customer service.

Our Internet service is rarely interrupted and the majority of the problems that do occur are repaired within one hour. We consider every Internet interruption to be an emergency. This year, most customers who left *SuperMegaTech* returned to our company within two months because they had experienced more problems with the new cut-rate companies. The other companies have neither better quality nor better customer service. They just can't offer what we do: the best of both worlds! Most people who try *SuperMegaTech* realize that our superb service is worth a few dollars more each month. For a limited time only, we are offering your first month of personal Internet service at a 50% discount. So try us and see why more people are switching to *SuperMegaTech* every day!

---

equipped: prepared; having the necessary equipment

1. There are many quantifiers in the leaflet that refer to large quantities of a noun. The first one has been circled. Find and circle six more.

2. There are some quantifiers in the leaflet that refer to a small quantity. The first one has been underlined. Find and underline at least one more.

3. The leaflet begins with a quantifier with *of*. Why did the writer use *of*? Check the correct answer.

   _____ a. The quantifier is talking about a specific noun.

   _____ b. This quantifier always appears with *of* before a noun.

2 **Contrasting Quantifiers**

Read the sentences and circle the best expression to complete each one.

1. I need ((more)/much) time to finish this project.

2. (A few/A little) people gave presentations in class.

3. He didn't like (either/neither) one.

4. (Some/Some of) my friends work from home.

5. How (many/much) food do we need?

6. I will e-mail you either today (or/nor) tomorrow.

7. We haven't seen (none/any) of those websites.

8. Melissa sees almost (every/both) new movie that comes out each year.

3 **Using Quantifiers with Specific and Nonspecific Nouns**

Read the following paragraphs and insert *of* after each quantifier where necessary.

A. These days a lot _____of_____ people use the Internet to pay their bills. Many _____
$_1$ $_2$
companies offer online billing and it has become very popular. Paying bills online is very easy.

One executive had this to say about online billing: "Some _____ our customers don't
$_3$

understand how to use online billing, but we plan to train every _____ customer who is
$_4$

interested in learning."

B. All _____ children in our community learn about computers in school. They must
$_1$

use computers each _____ day in order to complete their homework. However, fewer
$_2$

_____ elderly people in this area know how to use computers. We are hoping to help the
$_3$

elderly by offering plenty _____ computer classes at the senior citizen centers in town.
$_4$

C. Online dating is very popular in America these days. There are many _____ websites
$_1$

that introduce single people to one another. Several _____ these websites claim they
$_2$

have inspired a large number _____ weddings. Single people can create a profile on these
$_3$

websites and even post a few _____ pictures of themselves for prospective dates to see.
$_4$

4 **Combining Form, Meaning, and Use**

Read the following pairs of sentences. Write *S* if the sentences have the same meaning. Write *D* if their meanings are different. For the sentences that are different, change the *b* sentence so that it means the same as *a*.

___D___ 1. a. We have a little rice.

b. We have a large amount of rice.
    We have a small amount of rice.

_____ 2. a. The majority of the customers enjoyed the Internet demonstration.

b. Most of the customers enjoyed the Internet demonstration.

_____

_____ **3. a.** Few people were using e-mail in the early 1980s.

      b. Some people were using e-mail in the early 1980s.

      _____

_____ **4. a.** Every customer is important.

      b. Neither customer is important.

      _____

_____ **5. a.** Hardly any Internet users know about this website.

      b. Few Internet users know about this website.

      _____

_____ **6. a.** Plenty of people saw our advertisement.

      b. A small number of people saw our advertisement.

      _____

_____ **7. a.** I do not like e-mail and I do not like my cell phone.

      b. I like both e-mail and my cell phone.

      _____

_____ **8. a.** Almost all of the students were teenagers.

      b. Most of the students were teenagers.

      _____

5 Thinking About Meaning and Use

Read each sentence and the statements that follow. Circle the correct statement about the underlined words.

1. <u>Neither</u> of my sisters is married.
   a. The speaker has many sisters.
   b. The speaker has two sisters.

2. <u>Each</u> guest received a welcome gift from the company. This sentence refers to . . .
   a. all of the guests as a group.
   b. every guest as an individual.

3. Most students use the Internet frequently but <u>some</u> do not.
   a. *Some* refers to a large group of students.
   b. *Some* is used as a pronoun.

4. I do <u>a great deal of</u> my work from home. The speaker does . . .
   a. all of his work from home.
   b. a lot of his work from home.

5. We have <u>plenty of</u> time.
   a. We have enough time.
   b. We are worried about running out of time.

6. <u>All</u> customers want a good deal. This sentence refers to . . .
   a. customers in general.
   b. a specific group of customers.

7. I pay <u>the majority of</u> my bills online. The speaker pays . . .
   a. a few of her bills online.
   b. most of her bills online.

8. I spend <u>less</u> time e-mailing than you do. The speaker is . . .
   a. saying he spends a lot of time e-mailing.
   b. comparing his e-mail use with the listener's.

9. Shawn didn't eat <u>much</u> food tonight. Shawn must . . .
   a. have been hungry.
   b. not have been hungry.

10. <u>Some of</u> the homework was difficult. The speaker is talking about . . .
    a. part of the homework.
    b. all of the homework.

Read the information and complete the tasks.

Computer Use Statistics for Buftonville

This poll shows how the people we surveyed in Buftonville are using computers.

- 94% of people have used a computer.
- 85% of people use a computer at least once a week.
- 43% of people use a computer every day.
- 13% of people use computers for business only.
- 17% of people use computers for personal use only.
- 59% of people use computers for both business and personal reasons.
- 17% of computer users do not use the Internet at all.
- 27% of computer users use only the Internet and word processing software.
- 56% of computer users use the Internet and a variety of software.
- 89% of people have an e-mail account.
- 9% of people primarily communicate with their families by e-mail.

A. Write eight sentences about computer use in Buftonville. Use as many different quantifiers as possible.

1. _The majority of people use computers for both business and personal reasons._
2. _____
3. _____
4. _____
5. _____
6. _____
7. _____
8. _____

B. Use quantifiers to answer the following questions about your own computer use.

1. How much time do you spend on the Internet?

   I spend a great deal of time on the Internet.

2. How often do you use computers?

   _____

3. How many different software programs do you use?

   _____

4. How much e-mail do you send each week?

   _____

7 Contrasting Quantifiers Before Noncount or Plural Count Nouns

Read the following sentences. Write *N* if the underlined quantifier is used with a noncount noun. Write *P* if it is used with a plural count noun.

__P__ **1.** <u>Few</u> people have seen this new product.

_____ **2.** <u>A large number of</u> homes have cable Internet connections.

_____ **3.** Children spend <u>too much</u> time using computers.

_____ **4.** I need <u>a little</u> help learning how to use this program.

_____ **5.** <u>Hardly any of</u> my friends understood the question.

_____ **6.** I found <u>some</u> information on this website.

_____ **7.** <u>Many</u> college courses require students to use computers.

_____ **8.** Online shopping saves me <u>lots of</u> money.

_____ **9.** <u>Several</u> professors asked us the same thing.

_____ **10.** <u>Some</u> friends visited Robert at work today.

8 Editing Nouns

Find and correct the errors. The first one has been corrected for you.

Lori: Hey, Kenny! Can I use your computer later today?

Kenny: I don't know. I have a ~~lots~~ *lot* of work to do today. How much do you have to do?

Lori: Oh, I don't have a very large number of work to do. I only need it for a little while.

Kenny: Why don't you use a computer lab on campus? Most of buildings have a computer lab.

Lori: I know. My dorm has two, but neither one isn't open today.

Kenny: Neither computer lab are open? That's weird. Are you sure?

Lori: Yes, I'm sure. I spend quite a few time there. Most the time they work fine, but much computers were infected with a virus yesterday, so the labs are closed today.

Kenny: Oh, that's too bad. How many time will it take you to finish your work?

Lori: Only about twenty minutes. I already finished the majority of it.

Kenny: I think you can use my roommate's computer. I have a lot of homework but I don't think he has none.

Lori: Thank you so much! I'll come by later.

Follow the instructions to write a descriptive paragraph. Use the Writing Checklist to check your work.

Think about how you spend your time in an average day. Make a list showing how much time you spend on each activity. Think about these questions and make notes: Why do you spend your time this way? Why are these activities important or enjoyable? Could you be using your time in a better way? On a separate sheet of paper, use your notes to write a detailed paragraph about your daily life and the activities that you choose to do each day.

My daily life is very busy. I spend a lot of time taking care of my children but I try to spend as much time as possible doing studying for college, as well. Every day, I get together with several friends in the library and we help each other with our projects. At home, I try to spend time . . .

Writing Checklist

Reflect on your ability to use quantifiers by answering the questions.

☐ 1. Did you use quantifiers to describe singular, plural, and non-count of nouns?

☐ 2. Did you use pronouns or phrases with pronouns to replace some quantifiers?

☐ 3. Did you use comparative quantifiers?

☐ 4. Did you use quantifiers in combination with other modifiers?

☐ 5. Did you check for subject-verb agreement with determiners and *of* phrases?

9 Gerunds and Infinitives

FORM, MEANING, AND USE

 Examining Form

Read this office memo and complete the tasks.

To: All employees
From: Bill Wiley, CEO and President
Date: October 17
Re: Upcoming overtime

    I don't like to work late every day. I don't like my employees <u>working</u> late every day, either. Unfortunately, it will be necessary for everyone to pitch in and work overtime during the month of November. Our company's workload is at an all-time high, and it will continue to increase throughout next month. We will hire three new employees by the end of November, but in the meantime everyone will need to pull together in order to ensure that our company standards are maintained. Of course, working late all month will be a burden on you and your families. I understand that and I want you to know that I appreciate your dedication to this company. That is why all employees will receive an extra thousand dollars in their holiday bonus checks. This extra money is your compensation for dedicating so much time to your job this year. This company has grown very quickly over the past five years. I recognize that without you, we would not be a success. I believe that by caring for our employees, we will create a happy and productive workplace. I will expect you all to work hard this next month. However, making this work pleasant will be my top priority. For this reason, I also plan to provide food for those who stay late. Thank you all for agreeing to work overtime next month.

Sincerely,
Bill Wiley, CEO and President

---

to pitch in: to work together toward a common goal
compensation: payment or reward

to ensure: to make sure
burden: something that is oppressive or causes problems

1. Circle five examples of infinitives in the memo.

2. Underline five examples of gerunds in the memo.

3. Look at infinitives and gerund in the first three sentences. Who performs the actions described by the infinitives or gerund? Write the performer of each action on the lines below.

    a. _____

    b. _____

    c. _____

Circle the gerund or infinitive form to complete each sentence.

1. I hope (getting/(to get)) an interview.

2. He quit (going/to go) to that restaurant after he got food poisoning.

3. The Internet is useful for (finding/to find) quotations.

4. I expect them (making/to make) a lot of money.

5. Please remember (completing/to complete) your homework tonight.

6. Roger's (eating/to eat) lunch out every day costs us a lot of money.

7. She's in charge of (finding/to find) errors in the reports.

8. They are afraid (quitting/to quit) their jobs.

9. It is important (doing/to do) your best at work.

10. I have decided (helping/to help) you find a new job.

11. We had to move in order (getting/to get) good jobs.

12. She finally stopped (worrying/to worry) about the future.

3 Identifying the Performer of the Action

Underline the gerund or infinitive in each sentence. Then write *T* for true or *F* for false next to the statement that follows.

1. We don't want him to leave.

    __F__   We don't want to leave.

2. I intend to buy a new computer.

    _____   Someone will buy a new computer for me.

3. It is difficult for the managers to enforce this policy.

    _____   The managers enforce the policy.

4. I expect you to do well in this job.

    _____   I will do well in this job.

5. Some employees like working overtime.

    _____   Some employees work overtime.

6. Nobody can stand her bragging anymore.

    _____   She doesn't brag anymore.

7. It is better for him to know the truth.

    _____   Someone should tell him the truth.

8. We prefer eating dinner at home.

    _____   We like to eat dinner at home.

9. It is important to laugh every day.

    _____   People should laugh every day.

10. I can't wait to hear from you.

    _____   I want you to get in touch with me.

A. Read the chart. It shows some activities that Phil did this week. Complete the statements Phil would make about his activities. Use gerunds and infinitives.

ACTIVITY	AMOUNT OF TIME
Watched TV	Fourteen hours
Read the book *You Can Speak Spanish*	Three hours
Smoked	Zero minutes
Talked on the phone	Twenty minutes
Jogged in the park	Two hours
Wrote an essay for History 430	Eleven hours

1. I enjoy <u>watching TV</u>. I do it for at least two hours each day.
2. _____ is boring. I only did it for twenty minutes this week.
3. I spent a lot of time _____ this week. That class is really difficult.
4. I want to learn how _____, so I am reading a book about it.
5. I like _____ because it keeps me healthy. I do it for thirty minutes, four times a week.
6. I finally quit _____. I didn't do it at all this week.

B. Now complete the statements about your own life. Use gerunds and infinitives.

1. I enjoy _____.
2. _____ is boring.
3. I spent a lot of time _____ this week.
4. I want to learn how _____.
5. I like _____.
6. I finally quit _____.

C. Write some more statements about your own life using gerunds and infinitives.

1. <u>My favorite activity is hiking.</u>
2. _____
3. _____
4. _____

There are two situations in each of the following sentences. Write *1* by the earlier situation and *2* by the later situation.

1. They are reported to have sold one quarter of their stock.

    <u>2</u> a. It was reported.   <u>1</u> b. They sold one quarter of their stock.

2. We regretted having lied about the problem.

    _____ a. We felt regret.   _____ b. We lied about the problem.

3. After missing her instructor's phone call, Lila burst into tears.

    _____ a. Lila missed her instructor's phone call. _____ b. Lila cried.

4. They are known to have helped many people.

    _____ a. It was known.   _____ b. They helped many people.

6) Identifying Uses of Gerunds and Infinitives

Read the following sentences and complete the activities.

1. Underline the gerund or infinitive in each sentence. Then write *S* if the gerunds and infinitives are used as subjects and write *SC* if they are used as subject complements.

   __SC__ a. My hobby is <u>sketching</u>.

   _____ b. Doing yoga is very beneficial.

   _____ c. His plan is to take that class next semester.

   _____ d. Abby's favorite activity is dancing.

   _____ e. Training will begin tomorrow morning at 8:00 A.M.

2. Underline the gerund or infinitive in each sentence. Then write *OV* if the gerunds and infinitives are used as objects of verbs and write *OP* if they are used as objects of prepositions.

   __OV__ a. I hate <u>causing</u> trouble.

   _____ b. We plan to give everyone a raise.

   _____ c. I don't believe in working too hard.

   _____ d. Some people learn best by reading aloud.

   _____ e. We hope to finish the project before the holidays.

7) Using Passive Gerunds and Infinitives

Rewrite the following active sentences as passive sentences.

1. I don't like people calling me at work
   <u>I don't like being called at work.</u>

2. Someone needs to finish this report.
   _____

3. We enjoy people asking for our advice.
   _____

4. Ron prefers people to give him detailed instructions.
   _____

5. Someone has to install a new network immediately.
   _____

8) Understanding Verbs Followed by Both Gerunds and Infinitives

Place a check (✓) next to every appropriate response to each question or statement. There may be more than one appropriate response.

1. Can you watch my dog while I'm on vacation?

   __✓__ a. Sure! I love taking care of animals.

   __✓__ b. Sure! I love to take care of animals.

2. We have new carpeting in the house.

   _____ a. Don't worry. I'll remember to take my shoes off.

   _____ b. Don't worry. I'll remember taking my shoes off.

3. How can I help you?

   _____ a. You can continue answering the phone this afternoon.

   _____ b. You can continue to answer the phone this afternoon.

4. Why have you come home late every day this week?

_____ a. The boss has started giving us more work.

_____ b. The boss has started to give us more work.

5. Please turn off the lights before you leave.

_____ a. OK. And I won't forget locking the door, either.

_____ b. OK. And I won't forget to lock the door, either.

6. How can I save money this year?

_____ a. You can stop buying an expensive cup of coffee every day.

_____ b. You can stop to buy an expensive cup of coffee every day.

9 Editing

Find and correct the errors. The first one has been corrected for you.

Ask Nancy

Dear Nancy,

I have a problem and I'm hoping you can help me decide what ~~doing~~ _to do_. My job has been very demanding lately and my husband has been unhappy because I've been working so much overtime. I don't mind working so much because I really like my job, but I do feel very tired after to work so many long hours. My husband wants me to work less and I agreed to stop to accept overtime assignments this month. The problem is that now my boss is requiring every employee to work overtime for the whole month of November. He is giving us an extra large holiday bonus, but my husband is very unhappy. He wants me to quit my job, but working are very important to me. What should I do?

Sincerely,

Confused

Dear Confused,

It sounds as if you are stuck between a rock and a hard place. You like working and to spend time with your colleagues, but you also like having a happy home. You shouldn't quit to work, but you need to find a solution. First, it is essential to talk to your husband. He probably does not you want to be fired or reprimanded at work. He just wants spending more time with you. You can make your situation at home better by to talk to your husband and telling him that you understand how he feels. You can let him know that you want to spend time with him, but that your job is very important to you as well. You must also talk to your boss. It is important to let him know that you are unhappy about being not given a choice regarding the overtime hours in November. Maybe his plan is to require the overtime now and gives extra time off in January, for example. By talking with your boss, there may be a chance to compromise.

Sincerely,

Nancy

Follow the instructions to write two paragraphs that describe your attitudes towards work. Use gerunds and infinitives as appropriate. Then use the Writing Checklist to check your work.

In the first paragraph, write about your attitudes toward work in general. Is work important to you? Do you think it should occupy a lot of time? Is it necessary to be passionate about the work you do? Why or why not? How much work is too much? If a job is stressful, is it better to quit? What is the most important feature of a good job? What makes a job unacceptable? In the second paragraph, write about your current job. Where do you work? What kind of work do you do? Do you work long hours? What time of day do you usually work? Is your job stressful? Why or why not? What would you like to change about your job?

Having an enjoyable and interesting job is very important. Working takes up a lot of our time, so it is necessary to do something that is stimulating and rewarding.

Writing Checklist

Reflect on your ability to use gerunds and infinitives by answering the questions.

☐ 1. Did you use gerunds and infinitives to talk about actions and states?

☐ 2. Did you use pronouns to replace gerund or infinitive phrases?

☐ 3. Did you use summarizing nouns to replace gerund or infinitive phrases?

☐ 4. Did you use any verbs in the passive followed by an infinitive?

☐ 5. Did you check your sentences for correct form?

Chapters 7–9

A. Insert *a*, *an*, or *the* where appropriate. If an article shouldn't be in the sentence, cross it out or change it to an appropriate one.

1. Your bag is in kitchen and please don't forget to take laptop today!
2. The love at first sight is totally ridiculous idea.
3. Susan, could you feed dog, please? Poor Dunbar looks hungry.
4. The car I want costs thousand dollars more than I can afford.
5. I can recommend great restaurant in Rome. It's right on river.
6. Let me give you piece of the advice – never chase a lion.
7. You'll find the bank on left just past store called *SmartMart*.
8. That's weird! There are a policemen in your apartment.
9. Do you want chicken, the beef, or a fish for dinner tonight?
10. Ryoko had awful headache so she left the office and went home.

B. Circle all the possible words or phrases to complete each sentence.

11. _____ students passed the exam. It was too difficult.
    a. Very little
    b. Very few
    c. None
    d. Hardly any
12. You really should try _____ this apple tart. It's delicious!
    a. a great deal of
    b. a little of
    c. some of
    d. most of
13. In my opinion, _____ sales or marketing should come up with a plan.
    a. neither
    b. either
    c. nor
    d. both
14. _____ my professors are interested in astrophysics.
    a. Each
    b. Both
    c. Every
    d. All

15. The law states that _____ child should get an equal chance in life.
    a. every
    b. some
    c. all
    d. neither

16. _____ people would disagree with you.
    a. Most
    b. A few
    c. Few
    d. Some

17. Why do _____ students want to take the psychology course this year?
    a. a great deal of
    b. so few
    c. so many
    d. so little

18. _____ of my time is spent managing people.
    a. Hardly any
    b. Any
    c. Much
    d. Lots

C. Choose the correct words or phrases.
    19. My boss always avoids (to have/having) an argument.
    20. I have difficulty (finding/to find) time for leisure activities.
    21. It's impossible for me (getting/to get) a raise in this company!
    22. Most people dislike (to see/seeing) cruelty to animals.
    23. We were hungry so we stopped (buying/to buy) a snack.
    24. I really hope (to pass/passing) my driver's test.
    25. The lecturer urged students (presenting/to present) their papers.
    26. Did you remember (saying/to say) thank you for the meal?
    27. (Bob/Bob's) working late annoys his wife.
    28. Kathy doesn't mind (to help/helping) us.
    29. They plan on (calling/to call) after the interview.
    30. Promise me (coming back/to come back) later.

CHAPTER

10 Relative Clauses and Adjective Phrases

FORM, MEANING, AND USE

1 Examining Form

Read this article and complete the tasks.

Leonardo da Vinci

Leonardo da Vinci was a man *who personified the Italian Renaissance.* The Renaissance, which took place in the 15th and 16th centuries, was a time of great creativity and invention. You may have heard the term "renaissance man." A renaissance man is someone who has many different skills and seems to be able to do anything well. Leonardo da Vinci is a great example of a renaissance man.

Da Vinci was an artist, writer, scientist, and inventor. He was a brilliant man whose ideas were far ahead of his time. In fact, some people have even suggested he was an alien! He probably wasn't an alien, but he did make detailed drawings of things that we think of as modern inventions. For example, he drew plans for a helicopter and for contact lenses in a time when there was no electricity or plastic. Of course, these items were not produced until centuries after his death.

Most people today recognize Leonardo da Vinci mainly for his artwork. He painted The Last Supper *fresco* in Milan, as well as many famous portraits. His most famous painting is The Mona Lisa, *which now hangs in the Louvre in Paris.*

---

personified: embodied, represented
ahead of his time: futuristic, more closely related to the future than the present
portrait: painting of a person
alien: a creature from outer space

1. Circle eight examples of relative clauses in the article.

2. How many of the relative clauses you circled are restrictive relative clauses?
   a. Put a star (★) next to those clauses.

3. How many of the relative clauses you circled are nonrestrictive relative clauses?
   a. Draw a check (✓) next to those clauses.

2 Omitting Relative Pronouns

Read the sentences. Underline each relative clause, then put parentheses around the relative pronoun if it can be omitted with no change in meaning. There may be more than one relative clause in each sentence.

1. Jack is the man (who) I work with that likes to ski.

2. Thomas Edison was the man who invented the light bulb.

3. That was the movie that we saw last year that was so terrible.

4. I just got a brochure for the car that I want to buy.

5. Why don't we go see the exhibit that you are so interested in?

6. Seattle is the city that is famous for its coffee.

7. My boyfriend found the birthday present that I hid under the couch!

8. Lori is the lady that you met who I went to high school with.

3 Using Relative Pronouns

Complete this dialogue by circling the correct relative pronoun(s) in parentheses. More than one relative pronoun may be possible in each sentence.

Amanda: Hey, who is the guy (who/whose/Ø) helped you with your math homework?
                                    1

David: Oh, that was Bill. He's the one (who/that/Ø) came to our Superbowl party.
                                              2

Amanda: Oh, right! He was the guy (which/who/where) was wearing a green hat.
                                        3

David: Yeah, that's him. He helped me with the homework (which/that/who) was due last week. I'm taking
                                                              4
the same math class (that/Ø/when) he took last semester.
                     5

Amanda: That's the class (Ø/that/which) Professor Kelly teaches, right?
                              6

David: Yes, and he is the professor (whose/who/that) homework assignments are very difficult. I was failing
                                        7
the class, so I had to get help from somebody (who/which/Ø) understood it.
                                               8

Amanda: Everybody has at least one subject (that/who/Ø) is especially difficult. Remember when I took that
                                               9
literature class? I had to find a tutor, and I ended up doing well.

David: Yeah, I remember that. You took that class in the same building (when/that/where) I worked at the time.
                                                                            10

Amanda: That's right! I forgot about that.

4 Working on Subject and Object Relative Clauses

Choose the best option to complete each sentence.

1. I married the man that (I fell in love with/fell in love with).

2. Brenda never met the people who (work/works) in the office.

3. Athletes should eat the foods that (they give/give) them the most energy.

4. We didn't recognize the men who Carolina (was/were) eating with.

5. Juan only takes classes that (are/they are) easy.

6. Everyone clapped for the actress who (she played/played) the lead role.

7. I just met the professor that (we heard about/heard about).

8. Michael will apply for the jobs that he (see/sees) advertised in today's paper.

9. Julia won't eat any food that (didn't cook/she didn't cook) herself.

10. I love the sauce that (I tasted/tasted) of almonds.

5 **Understanding Restrictive versus Nonrestrictive Relative Clauses**

Read the sentences below. Underline the relative clauses and decide whether they are restrictive or nonrestrictive relative clauses. Then write a comma before and after each nonrestrictive relative clause, where appropriate.

1. Last summer, when I went to Brazil, was the happiest time of my life.

2. 1977 was the year when Elvis died.

3. Let's talk about the reason why you are here.

4. Willie Perdomo who is a famous poet spoke at our school.

5. Patrick is interested in dating the girl who sits in the front row.

6. Buenos Aires where I spent my childhood is a beautiful city.

7. Would you like some of the cookies that I baked?

8. Jimmy is working with Ali whose brother attends my church.

9. *Catch-22* which is my favorite book was written by Joseph Heller.

10. What do you think about the paper that I wrote?

6 **Combining Sentences Using Relative Clauses**

Read the sentences below. Combine each pair of sentences into one sentence. Use restrictive and nonrestrictive relative clauses where appropriate.

1. Yesterday I saw a man. The man tried to steal apples from the supermarket.
   Yesterday I saw a man who tried to steal apples from the supermarket.

2. Rosa and Paul are coming to the party. They moved into the neighborhood last week.
   _____
   _____

3. Veronica said she can get us tickets to the game. She is married to a baseball player.
   _____
   _____

4. My friends met a woman. The woman escaped the *Titanic* in a lifeboat.
   _____
   _____

5. We finally saw the movie. You told us to see the movie.
   _____
   _____

6. Anna Maria can't go until Saturday. She doesn't have to work on Saturday.
   _____
   _____

7. I really like the book. Linda wrote the book.
   _____
   _____

Read the following pairs of sentences. Write *S* if the sentences have the same meaning. Write *D* if their meanings are different.

__S__ 1. **a.** Diane's boyfriend, who knew she was joking, began to laugh.

      b. Diane's boyfriend, knowing she was joking, began to laugh.

_____ 2. **a.** The man who lives next door is very friendly.

      b. The man living next door is very friendly.

_____ 3. **a.** We followed the signs that directed us to the exhibition.

      b. We followed the signs directing us to the exhibition.

_____ 4. **a.** Anyone who requires assistance should notify the flight attendant.

      b. Anyone requiring assistance should notify the flight attendant.

_____ 5. **a.** I'm talking to someone who makes sushi.

      b. I'm talking to someone making sushi.

_____ 6. **a.** The students, who knew the exam would be difficult, felt nervous.

      b. The students, knowing the exam would be difficult, felt nervous.

_____ 7. **a.** Look at the student playing the piano.

      b. Look at the student who plays the piano.

_____ 8. **a.** The property which was destroyed will be replaced.

      b. The property being destroyed will be replaced.

Rewrite the sentences below so that they contain adjective phrases instead of relative clauses, when possible. If it isn't possible to change the relative clause to an adjective phrase, write *Not possible* on the line.

1. The students who are in the next classroom are very noisy.
   The students in the next classroom are very noisy.

2. The oysters that were served in this restaurant made many people sick.
   _____

3. Mrs. Thornton, who seems so unpleasant, actually spends a lot of time helping the poor people in this town.
   _____

4. Manette Edwards, who is my coworker, just got married in Las Vegas.
   _____

5. The song that we were listening to is a classic.
   _____

6. A box that weighed twenty pounds fell on my foot.
   _____

7. We had to spend all night in a room that was cold.
   _____

8. Sorry I'm late. I stopped to help someone who was having car problems.
   _____

Find and correct the errors. The first one has been corrected for you.

Getting to know Brandy Jones.

You all know Brandy Jones for her many wonderful inventions that *have* ~~has~~ made parenting so much easier. Last month our magazine printed an article titled, *Oh, Baby!*, praised Ms. Jones' latest invention, an easy-to-use car seat for infants. This month, I had a chance to sit down with Ms. Jones, whose inventions has revolutionized our lives.

Reporter: I can't believe I'm sitting here with the woman, who invented the best car seat ever made! I love your new car seat, but that's not even the invention you're most famous.

Ms. Jones: Thank you so much. You're right. The invention is most popular is probably the SuperFast Stroller.

Reporter: Absolutely! How do you come up with your ideas?

Ms. Jones: Whenever I see mothers seeming stressed out, I wonder about the reason which they look that way. I wonder what I can do to help. I remember feeling so stressed out in the early 1980s when my children were still very young. That was about the time when I invented my stroller, who was like nothing I had seen in the stores.

---

10 Writing

Follow the instructions to write a descriptive paragraph. Use the Writing Checklist to check your work.

Think about a product you would like someone to invent. Why do you need this product? What would it do? What problem in your life would it help you solve? List some of the features you would like it to have. Then write notes describing the product. On a separate sheet of paper, use your notes to write a detailed paragraph imagining that you have invented this product. Use relative clauses and adjective phrases to describe the product.

I have just invented a coffee maker that makes two different kinds of coffee. My roommate, who drinks decaffeinated coffee, used to have his own coffee maker, so we could both drink our coffee in the morning. Having two coffee makers took up a lot of space on the counter, which isn't very large. The coffee maker I invented has . . .

Writing Checklist

Reflect on your ability to use articles by answering the questions.

☐ 1. Did you use subject and object relative clauses to introduce, define, or identify nouns?

☐ 2. Did you use nonrestrictive relative clauses to add background information?

☐ 3. Did you use relative clauses with other relative pronouns (*whose, where, when*)?

☐ 4. Did you use any adjective phrases?

☐ 5. Did you check your sentences for correct form?

11 Coordinating Conjunctions and Transitions

FORM, MEANING, AND USE

 1 Examining Form

Read this magazine article and complete the tasks below.

Gratitude and forgiveness

It seems as if happiness is hard to find these days. Everyone is looking for it, but very few people seem to have actually found it. Many people expect to find happiness in the world around them, so they search for money, power, and fame to make them happy. If we look at modern day celebrities, <u>however</u>, we can see that these things do not bring happiness. In fact, as the tabloids tell us, they often bring considerable unhappiness and pain. Why, then, do so many people continue to see wealth, power, and fame as the key to contentment?

The latest research, on the other hand, presents a different view of happiness. It suggests that the best way to be happier is to look within ourselves and try to change our behavior. More specifically, we need to cultivate gratitude and forgiveness. Studies show that people who work to strengthen these two feelings report more contentment in their daily lives. Moreover, people who find it difficult to forgive others have a much higher rate of heart disease. Researchers suggest, therefore, that everyone look for ways to be more grateful and forgiving. For example, we can all spend time each evening thinking about the positive events of the day, so we can feel more grateful for the good things in our lives. We can practice forgiveness by ignoring the small transgressions of others. For instance, if a driver cuts us off in traffic, we can choose to let it go rather than get upset. If we practice this in such instances, we might find it easier to forgive someone for a more serious offense. Practicing gratitude and forgiveness is good for us and great for society as a whole!

---

cultivate: grow, nourish   **transgressions:** wrongdoings, offenses

1. Circle five examples of coordinating conjunctions in the article.

2. Underline five examples of transitions in the article.

3. What are the functions of the coordinating conjunctions in this article? Put a check (✓) **for each** correct answers.

   _____ a. Showing additional ideas

   _____ b. Showing contrast between ideas

   _____ c. Showing alternative ideas

   _____ d. Showing a result

2 Contrasting Coordinating Conjunctions and Transitions

Complete the following sentences by circling the most appropriate coordinating conjunction or transition in parentheses.

1. I try to get a lot of exercise. (On the contrary/For instance), I jog for thirty minutes every morning.

2. Our employees are all highly qualified and have a great deal of experience. (Moreover/Instead), we require them to complete an extensive training program after they are hired.

3. Testing medicine on animals can save many human lives. (In spite of this/In addition), many researchers avoid animal testing when possible because it harms so many animals.

4. We can continue fighting, (but/or) we can learn to get along at work.

5. Elephants live in groups with a well-established pecking order. (Similarly/Consequently), most corporations have a very clear chain of command.

6. Many chimpanzees learn very quickly (so/and) imitate human behavior.

3 Understanding Transitions

A. Decide why the transition in each of the following sentences is used. Choose the correct reason from the box and write it on the line.

> a. The transition is used to show an additional idea.
>
> b. The transition is used to contrast between ideas.
>
> c. The transition is used to show sequence or organize ideas.

_a_ 1. Horses and zebras are very similar animals. They are, in fact, related.

_____ 2. It's easy to talk about conflict resolution in the work place. It's much more difficult to practice it on a daily basis, however.

_____ 3. Working at the zoo has provided me with many skills and valuable experiences. Furthermore, it's the most enjoyable job I've ever had.

_____ 4. Right now I'm taking classes to fulfill the basic requirements for my degree. After this, I'll begin taking specialized classes in zoology.

_____ 5. I'm thinking of studying the Quechua language because I find it intriguing. On the other hand, I might not have an opportunity to use the language very much in this city.

_____ 6. Spiders are fascinating animals that create beautiful patterns in their webs. In addition, they eat the insects that bother us so much.

B. Decide why the transition in each of the following sentences is used. Choose the correct reason from the box and write it on the line.

> a. The transition is used to show a similar idea.
>
> b. The transition is used to show a result.
>
> c. The transition is used to show a time relationship.

_c_ 1. The students are having a difficult time working together on this project. We'll let them try to work it out without any interference for now.

_____ 2. The employees have been spending a lot of time fighting lately. As a result, they haven't gotten anything done.

_____ **3.** Howler monkeys spend most of their lives in the treetops of the rainforest. <u>Likewise</u>, the three-toed sloth rarely touches the ground.

_____ **4.** Gena's boyfriend took her to see a movie. <u>Meanwhile</u>, we prepared the house for her surprise party.

_____ **5.** We need to check into our hotel room right away. <u>Afterwards</u>, we can go downstairs and explore the city.

_____ **6.** This project is very important to me. I will, <u>therefore</u>, be spending a lot of time working on it.

4 Combining Form, Meaning, and Use

Read the following pairs of sentences. Write *S* if the sentences have the same meaning. Write *D* if their meanings are different. For the sentences that are different, change the *b* sentence so that it means the same as *a*, but use a different transition or conjunction.

_D_ **1. a.** The party has been fun. Nevertheless, it's time to go home.

    b. The party has been fun. Most importantly, it's time to go home.
    <u>The party has been fun. Even so, it's time to go home.</u>

_____ **2. a.** We have a lot to discuss at this meeting. First, let's talk about last month's sales.

    b. We have a lot to discuss at this meeting. To begin, let's talk about last month's sales.

_____ **3. a.** Lions travel in groups. Wolves, on the other hand, travel alone.

    b. Lions travel in groups. Wolves, as a result, travel alone.

_____ **4. a.** The movie was interesting, but it was too long.

    b. The movie was interesting, for it was too long.

_____ **5. a.** Some animals can be more dangerous than they appear. For instance, many people are killed by hippos each year.

    b. Some animals can be more dangerous than they appear. However, many people are killed by hippos each year.

_____ **6. a.** Ron and Brenda plan to spend the first day of their vacation on the beach. Afterwards, they will go shopping.

    b. Ron and Brenda plan to spend the first day of their vacation on the beach. Then, they will go shopping.

5 Combining Sentences with Coordinating Conjunctions

Read the sentences below. Combine each pair of sentences into one sentence using a coordinating conjunction. Omit the subject and auxiliary verb in the second clause where possible.

1. He may be very tired. He may just be very lazy.
    <u>He may be very tired or just very lazy.</u>

2. Miranda apologized. Frank didn't care.

3. We ate dinner in a nice restaurant. We saw a funny movie.

4. We arrived at the meeting late. We had to sit in the back row.

_____

5. The birds were flying through the air. The birds were making a lot of noise.

_____

6. Did he call you? Did you call him?

_____

6) Connecting Sentences with Transitions

Read the sentences below. Connect each pair of sentences using an appropriate transition.

1. If you accept this job, you have to answer the phone and greet the clients. You have to bring me my mail every afternoon.
   If you accept this job, you have to answer the phone and greet the clients.
   In addition, you have to bring me my mail every afternoon.

2. Many baseball players come from Latin America. Sammy Sosa is from the Dominican Republic.

_____
_____

3. Bob stole money from his employer. He was fired.

_____
_____

4. Roberta does not like children at all. She refuses to go to a party if children will be there.

_____
_____

5. Our conflict resolution training can make your workplace more pleasant. It can improve your productivity.

_____
_____

6. Mr. Johnson is not stingy at all. He is the most generous man in the neighborhood.

_____
_____

7) Thinking About Meaning and Use

Choose the best answer to complete each sentence.

1. My wife is very nice to everyone and __a__.
   a. she has many friends
   b. her mother taught her to be kind

2. We go to Washington, D.C. for the Independence Day celebration every year, for _____.
   a. we saw our friend Angie there this year
   b. it's always so festive there

3. Ferrets are very solitary animals. Similarly, _____.
   a. cats prefer spending time alone
   b. dogs hate spending time alone

4. We want our children to get along better. As a matter of fact, _____.
   a. they go to school all day
   b. we are going to take them to a counselor

5. First, he answered the phone. Then, _____.
   a. the phone rang
   b. he heard a familiar voice on the line

6. The concert was sold out, for _____.
   a. we went to see a different show
   b. the band is very popular

Find and correct the errors. The first one has been corrected for you.

To:	All employees
From:	Brad Reynolds
Subject:	Conflict in the workplace

Dear Employees,

    I am disappointed to be receiving so many reports of serious conflicts amongst the employees of this company. I have worked as the human resources director for many years ~~for~~ *and* it is my job to handle such complaints. Similarly, I have never seen this many complaints in any one three-month period. I usually receive very, on the contrary, few reports of workplace conflict. Our company has been an enjoyable place to work for over a decade, however, the past three months have been much different. The prospect of losing jobs is scary, but I want you to know that the downsizing is just a rumor, though. Our, in fact, new CEO has promised us that there will be no downsizing for at least one full year. Your jobs are all safe moreover, and everyone will be receiving a raise in January. Thank you for your hard work.

– B. Reynolds

Follow the instructions to write two paragraphs that describe your attitudes towards conflict in the workplace. Use coordinating conjunctions and transitions as appropriate. Then use the Writing Checklist to check your work.

In the first paragraph, write about your attitudes toward workplace conflict in general. Why or why not? Why do disputes happen in the workplace? What problems have you had with your coworkers in the past? What negative effects does conflict have in the workplace? Can it ever have a positive effect? In the second paragraph, write about your attitudes toward conflict resolution. What should be done when conflict happens in the workplace? Do you think it is the employer's responsibility to settle disputes between coworkers?

Workplace conflict is one of the biggest problems our businesses face today and we must find a way to reduce it. When employees have major disagreements, everyone suffers.

Writing Checklist

Reflect on your ability to use conjunctions and transitions by answering the questions.

☐ 1. Did you check to make sure your conjunctions and transitions express the relationship that you intend?

☐ 2. Did you use conjunctions to connect closely related supporting ideas?

☐ 3. Did you delete repeated subjects and auxiliary forms after conjunctions?

☐ 4. Did you use transitions to show a shift to a new idea?

☐ 5. Did you check for correct punctuation?

12 Adverb Clauses and Adverb Phrases

FORM, MEANING, AND USE

1 Examining Form

Read this article and complete the tasks below.

Climbing the Sacred Mountain

With a summit of 12,388 feet (3,776 meters), Mt. Fuji is Japan's tallest mountain. Since ancient times, this mountain has been a sacred place in both the Buddhist and Shinto religions. It is covered in snow for most of the year, but is free of snow during the official climbing season in July and August. <u>Although climbing this mountain is quite difficult</u>, hundreds of thousands of people, including grandparents and small children, make the journey to the top each year. The climb is dangerous <u>since Mt. Fuji is an active volcano with rather unpredictable weather</u>. The locals like to say that the mountain makes its own weather because conditions may change drastically in just a few minutes. Some people get hypothermia and altitude sickness <u>while attempting to climb the mountain</u>. Most people, however, enjoy an unforgettable experience on the mountain.

There are several trails that lead to the summit of Mt. Fuji. The most popular trails have simple mountain huts along the way that provide climbers with restrooms, food, water, and shelter. Most climbers carry tall wooden sticks <u>in order to maintain their balance and aid in the climb</u>. They also carry rain gear <u>so that they will be prepared for the unpredictable weather</u>. Warm clothing is essential <u>because the temperature can be very cold near the top of the mountain</u>, even in the summer months. Most climbers try to see the sunrise from the top of the mountain and may climb all through the night to achieve this goal. <u>Though difficult</u>, climbing Mt. Fuji is truly worth the effort.

summit: highest point of a mountain
sacred: having religious or spiritual significance
hypothermia: dangerous condition caused by low body temperature
altitude sickness: headache and nausea often experienced at high elevations

Four adverb clauses and three adverb phrases have been underlined in this article. List them here:

Adverb clauses: _____

_____

_____

_____

Adverb phrases: _____

_____

_____

2 Contrasting Subordinators

Read the sentences below. Circle the subordinator in parentheses to complete each sentence logically.

1. I'm going back to school (so that/despite the fact that) I can complete my education.

2. (Because/By the time) they get here, we'll be ready to eat.

3. Alan never liked that song (while/until) he saw the music video.

4. Let's just stop (so that/anywhere) there is a gas station.

5. (Although/Since) I didn't like them, I ate all the cookies my grandma made me.

6. You have to read the book (in order to/by the time) understand the title.

7. We arrived fifteen minutes late (because/despite the fact that) John is never on time.

8. Kimiko was able to climb to the top of Mt. Fuji (so that/though) Yuuki had to turn back earlier.

3 Using Adjective Clauses

Complete these sentences with an appropriate form of the verb in parentheses. Pay attention to the time in the main clause. More than one answer is sometimes possible.

1. I never spoke English well until I _____took_____ (take) an English class at a community college.

2. While you _____ (repair) your car, I'm going to be working on my homework.

3. I worked overtime last Monday so that I _____ (can) leave early on Tuesday.

4. Everyone will have heard the news by the time we _____ (make) the announcement.

5. Though Kristiana _____ (know) the class would be difficult, she was surprised that there was so much homework.

6. My roomate always cooks dinner when he _____ (get) home from work.

7. They went to the new restaurant because they _____ (hear) the food was delicious.

8. Since you _____ (have) a new car, your insurance is going to go up.

4 Using Adverb Phrases

Rewrite the sentences below so that they contain adverb phrases instead of adverb clauses, when possible. If it isn't possible to change the adverb clause to an adverb phrase, write *Not possible*.

1. I'll be able to buy a new car after I get my bonus check.
   I'll be able to buy a new car after getting my bonus check.

2. Lori is learning to meditate so that she can reduce her anxiety.
   _____

3. My brothers have visited the Metropolitan Museum of Art ten times since they moved to New York.
   _____

4. As we had never met Maria's new boyfriend, we were surprised to hear that they had gotten engaged.
   _____

5. Though she is eating healthier food, she is still having a hard time losing weight.
   _____

6. While we are eating dinner, we can talk seriously about moving.
   _____

7. When Katie is working, her mom takes care of the children and prepares their meals.
   _____

Thinking About Meaning and Use

Read the statements that follow each sentence. Decide whether they are the same (S) or different (D).

1. I quit my job while looking for another one.

   __D__ Having quit my job, I looked for another one.

2. You can get your computer repaired anywhere this brand is sold.

   _____ This brand is sold wherever you want to get your computer repaired.

3. Since I wasn't paying attention, a car crashed into my truck.

   _____ A car crashed into my truck when I wasn't paying attention.

4. Having had some free time, Andrea and David went running.

   _____ Andrea and David went running whenever they had some free time.

5. She wants to climb Mt. Fuji since she's in such good shape.

   _____ Being in such good shape, she wants to climb Mt. Fuji.

6. Although he was sick, Joe couldn't miss work again.

   _____ Joe couldn't miss work again despite being sick.

7. I helped Jen so that she could learn the material.

   _____ I helped Jen in order to learn the material.

8. I always turn off the TV before working.

   _____ I never begin working until I turn off the TV.

6 **Writing Sentences with Adverb Clauses and Adverb Phrases**

Match the phrases from each column to write twelve logical sentences with adverb clauses or adverb phrases.

while	since	because	although	so that

Jonathan finally heard Madonna's new song	I wouldn't be nervous on exam day.
I studied a lot for the exam	there's a lot of traffic on the highway.
They were working on their homework yesterday	listening to the radio.
You have learned so many new words	I could save some money.
Carina called to say she'll be late	you are at your piano lesson.
I painted the walls myself	moving to this country.
We are going to the mall	he doesn't like pop music.
	Scott and Martha didn't study at all.
	she left her house ten minutes early.
	Kris installed the cabinets.
	taking this class.
	they wanted to finish the assignment early.
	they are having a sale.

1. _Jonathan finally heard Madonna's new song although he doesn't like pop music._

2. _____

3. _____

4. _____

5. _____

6. _____

7. _____

8. _____

9. _____

10. _____

11. _____

12. _____

7) Examining Adjective Phrases

Underline the adjective phrase in each of the sentences below. Decide what its purpose is and write it on the line.

> a. Showing time
> b. Giving reasons
> c. Showing concession

_b_ **1.** <u>Having heard this song many times</u>, I know all the words by heart.

_____ **2.** You will see many interesting items while touring the museum.

_____ **3.** Not knowing how to fix the sink, he will have to hire a plumber.

_____ **4.** Though not very practical, her new car was a lot of fun to drive.

_____ **5.** Since watching that movie, I can't stop thinking about it.

_____ **6.** Being so tired, she'll probably decide to stay home tonight.

Find and correct the errors. The first one has been corrected for you.

YOUR MEDICAL QUESTIONS ————————

Dear Dr. Morales,

Can you please tell me what a panic attack is? I've been having some strange feelings ~~although~~ *since* I was in a car accident last month. My sister thinks I may be having panic attacks. Because this never happened before the accident. What should I do?

Sincerely,

Matt

Dear Matt,

Panic attacks are a type of anxiety disorder affecting millions of Americans. Because having had panic attacks myself in the past, I am quite familiar with them. Panic disorder is genetic, but many people begin experiencing symptoms, only after they live through a traumatic event. Panic attacks can occur anywhere the sufferer may be wherever. Some people even have panic attacks as driving. Though panic attacks are scary they are not deadly. People with panic attacks may avoid leaving their homes in order avoid embarrassment. Panic attack sufferers often feel hopeless, but panic attacks can be treated with medicine and/or therapy. I hope you will see your doctor for diagnosis as soon as you will read this article.

Good luck!

Dr. Morales

Follow the instructions to write two paragraphs about how you achieved a goal. Use adverb clauses and adverb phrases as appropriate. Then use the Writing Checklist to check your work.

In the first paragraph, write about the goal in general. What was the goal? How did you become interested in it? Why was the goal important to you? How long had this been a goal of yours? Why was it challenging to reach this goal? In the second paragraph, write how you achieved the goal. What did you do to make the goal a reality? Did you work alone or with someone? How long did it take you to achieve the goal? Did you need any special equipment? Did you take any classes? How did you feel when you finally achieved your goal?

I have wanted to climb Mt. Hood since I was ten years old. At that age, I lived in New York City and knew very little about the outdoors. I saw a mountaineering show about Mt. Hood on TV and I fell in love with the idea because Mt. Hood seemed so beautiful and different from everything I knew. As I grew older, I never forgot about my dream of climbing Mt. Hood . . .

Writing Checklist

Reflect on your ability to use adverb clauses and adverb phrases by answering the questions.

- ☐ 1. Did you check to make sure your subordinators express the relationship that you intend?
- ☐ 2. Did you use adverb clauses to give background information?
- ☐ 3. Did you use adverb clauses to acknowledge other opinions?
- ☐ 4. Did you use adverb clauses to give reasons for your opinion?
- ☐ 5. Did you use adverb phrases to make your writing more concise?
- ☐ 6. Did you check your sentences for correct punctuation?

Chapters 10–12

A. Combine each pair of sentences using the second sentence in each pair to make either a restrictive or nonrestrictive relative clause.

1. There are office policies. You're expected to adhere to them.

   _____

2. The dog really did eat my homework. It's ironic.

   _____

3. Astronomy is a science. Many people are fascinated by it.

   _____

4. Jazz and theatre are two forms of entertainment. I enjoy them.

   _____

5. Phil's fortieth birthday was an event. He was dreading it.

   _____

6. Animal testing is an issue. Many of my friends are concerned about it.

   _____

7. My grandmother was 98 when she died. She was born in India.

   _____

8. That's the guy! I can never remember his name.

   _____

9. The package hasn't arrived yet. That means I'll be late getting home.

   _____

10. My brother was supposed to call me but he didn't. It was annoying.

    _____

B. Reduce the relative clauses in each sentence. Use an adjective phrase.

11. The company uses an accounting system that was developed in the UK.

    _____

12. There was a police announcement that ordered everyone to evacuate the building.

    _____

13. A rabbit that weighed 60 pounds made it into the *Guinness World Records*.

    _____

14. Jack, who knew there was a problem, took action at once.

    _____

15. Anyone who reads the article will know it's nonsense.

    _____

16. A system that allows tests to be generated automatically is now available.

    _____

17. Only students that are in a full-time program will be eligible for the grant.

    _____

18. This recipe is perfect for anyone who wants a quick, light meal.

    _____

19. Patrick, who is my brother, works for the government.

    _____

20. No one who arrives at the gate late will be allowed to board the flight.

    _____

C. Choose the correct word or phrase.

21. Dogs are highly sociable animals _____ cats, who are fiercely independent.
    a. similarly
    b. unlike
    c. like

22. I think I want to study French. _____, maybe Spanish is more useful.
    a. On the contrary
    b. On the other hand
    c. Additionally

23. _____ being cold and tired, we walked another five miles.
    a. Moreover
    b. However
    c. Despite

24. We're happy that you won the essay contest. _____, we want you to work harder.
    a. Similarly
    b. Nevertheless
    c. Likewise

25. Sonja was very hungry. _____, she ate all the food in my fridge.
    a. In fact
    b. In spite of this
    c. However

26. I've had lots of time to write my book, _____ it's still not finished.
    a. in addition
    b. yet
    c. moreover

27. The company over-budgeted this year. _____, we have plenty of money to spend on new software.
    a. Likewise
    b. Despite this
    c. As a result

28. Many projects may be canceled, _____ expect a lot of changes.
    a. or
    b. so
    c. yet

29. I'll be asleep _____ you come home.
    a. since
    b. by the time
    c. once

30. _____ he started the job, he's looked much happier.
    a. By the time
    b. Since
    c. While

31. I'm off to work _____ I feel sick.
    a. due to the fact
    b. even though
    c. whenever

32. You should relax more _____ reduce your stress levels.
    a. because
    b. as
    c. in order to

33. Joe is bad at sports, _____ Jane excels in almost all sports.
    a. while
    b. in any case
    c. even though

34. _____ living in New York, I learned a lot about life.
    a. During
    b. Since
    c. While

13 Conditionals

FORM, MEANING, AND USE

1 Examining Form

Read this interview and complete the tasks.

Face to Face with Albert Adams

Reporter: Mr. Adams, we've just received reports that you've officially announced your candidacy for mayor. Is that correct?

Mr. Adams: Yes, it is. I hope to be elected as this city's mayor in November.

Reporter: How would this city change if you were elected mayor?

Mr. Adams: Well, if elected, my first priority would be to reduce crime in the city. I would increase the city's police force by 10 percent.

Reporter: Unless you raise taxes, that will be impossible to pay for.

Mr. Adams: Well, safety is very important. Even if I have to raise taxes, I will protect the residents of our city.

Reporter: I see. What else do you want us to know about your policies?

Mr. Adams: Well, I will implement several environmentally friendly policies to reduce pollution in our city. This is urgent and it will require the cooperation of all citizens.

Reporter: What do you mean by that?

Mr. Adams: If every citizen helps out just a little bit, we will greatly reduce pollution in our city. These measures are long overdue. If more environmentally friendly policies had been implemented just fifteen years ago, we would have a much cleaner city today.

---

candidacy: the state of running for political office   **implement:** to carry out

1. Underline six conditional sentences.

2. How many of these sentences include an unreal conditional? _____

3. Find the sentence that contains a conditional but no *if* clause. Draw a circle around it. Why did the writer omit the *if* clause? Check all the correct answers.

    _____ a. The conditional meaning is implied.

    _____ b. The writer does not want to be redundant.

    _____ c. There is no possible *if* clause in this case.

2 Using Real Conditionals

Choose the best ending for each sentence below.

1. If I finish my work early, _____
2. When we take the 8:00 bus, _____
3. Unless you leave right now, _____
4. If the accident was really bad, _____
5. If you had to cancel, _____
6. When he waited until Sunday night to study, _____

a. the road could still be closed.
b. why didn't you call to let us know?
c. I'll take a walk outside.
d. you won't arrive on time.
e. he always had to stay up very late.
f. we arrive on campus at 8:30.

3 Thinking About Meaning and Use

Choose the correct response to each statement or question. There may be more than one correct answer for each.

1. "If I hadn't had a car accident, I never would have bought this wonderful new car." The speaker . . .
   a. did not have a car accident.
   b. is considering how things might have happened differently.
   c. had a car accident because he bought a new car.

2. "I'm going to drive to the conference even if the roads are bad." The speaker . . .
   a. will drive to the conference if the roads are bad.
   b. will drive to the conference if the roads are not bad.
   c. is certain that the roads will be bad.

3. "When my children get home from school, they have a snack and do their homework."
   The speaker is . . .
   a. talking about an unreal situation.
   b. not certain what her children do when they get home from school.
   c. talking about habitual actions.

4. "If the Earth were closer to the Sun, our planet would be too hot for human life." The speaker is . . .
   a. talking about a real situation.
   b. considering an imaginary situation.
   c. giving advice.

5. "The Tigers will probably win the World Series if their outfielders play well." The speaker is . . .
   a. talking about a habitual action.
   b. making a prediction.
   c. considering how things might have happened differently.

6. "If I had tried harder, I could have learned to play the guitar very well." The speaker . . .
   a. has never played the guitar.
   b. is considering how things might have happened differently.
   c. is talking about a real situation.

7. "If Zach gets a raise this year, he might get a better apartment." The speaker is . . .
   a. sure that Zach will get a raise.
   b. talking about a possible future event.
   c. talking about a timeless situation.

8. "If I were you, I'd apply for the job." The speaker is . . .
   a. giving advice.
   b. making a prediction.
   c. talking about a habitual action.

4 **Practicing Past Unreal Conditionals**

Write sentences using past unreal conditionals to answer the questions or respond to the statements below. Use the phrases in the box.

1. Why didn't you come to class? I was expecting to see you there.
   <u>I would have gone to class if I hadn't felt so sick.</u>

2. Why didn't you give Bob any money when he needed help?
   _____

3. I can't believe I am so busy this semester! I never have time to have fun.
   _____

4. Someone robbed my house this weekend. Do you think my neighbors saw the robber?
   _____

5. It's too bad Rosa didn't tell us she was having a problem with her workload.
   _____

6. I really wanted to go to the game, but it didn't work out. I guess it's for the best, right?
   _____

5 **Using Present and Future Unreal Conditionals**

Complete each sentence below with a logical clause.

1. If I found a hundred dollars, I would <u>take it to the police station</u>.

2. If I had more time, I could _____.

3. If I had a problem with one of my classmates, I would _____.

4. I would get so mad if _____.

5. If I were better at math, I would _____.

6. It sounds as if you are having trouble deciding whether to look for a new job.
   If I were you, I might _____.

7. Our noisy neighbors wouldn't bother us so much if _____.

6 **Understanding Real and Unreal Conditionals**

Choose the most appropriate response.

1. A: You'll never understand astronomy if you don't study.

   B: _____
      a. Then I won't study.
      b. So I guess I should study.

2. A: If I had been born in Quebec, I would be able to speak French.

   B: _____
      a. It's a shame you weren't born in Quebec.
      b. I'm glad you were born in Quebec.

3. A: If we're patient, we could see a shooting star.

   B: _____
      a. I'd like that very much.
      b. I didn't like that very much.

4. **A:** I would join a gym if I could afford the monthly fee.

   B: _____
      a. Well, that's good, so let's join.
      b. Don't feel bad. I can't join either.

5. **A:** If I had taken that class, I would know how to use this software.

   B: _____
      a. It's too bad you didn't.
      b. It's good you did.

6. **A:** If you're interested in modern art, you might like this exhibit.

   B: _____
      a. You're right. Maybe I will.
      b. You were right. I might have.

7. **A:** I'd like to see a movie tonight as long as I'm not too tired.

   B: _____
      a. OK. What time do you think will be best?
      b. I'm glad you won't be tired.

7   Editing

Find and correct the errors. The first one has been corrected for you.

Advice

Dear Randall,

I am having a problem with my astronomy class this semester. If you could help me decide what to do͵ I would really appreciate it. I overslept and missed the first test. Then I got a bad grade on the second test. When I had studied, I would have gotten a good grade. I totally forgot to study, though. There are still three tests left in the class. I think I could get a C if I will stay in the class. If I drop the class, I won't got a grade on my transcript at all. I am a sophomore and I have gotten either an A or a B in all my other classes. What would you do if you was me? Would you drop the class or just try to do better for the rest of the semester?

– Oops in Astronomy

Dear Oops,

First of all, if you will set your alarm clock, you would have made it to your first test. And if you had written your exam dates on a calendar. You might have remembered to study for your second test. If I were you I would learn to be more organized and responsible. I would also take fewer classes so I could concentrate better on each class. If I were in the exact situation you are in right now, I would have dropped the class and try again next semester.

– Randall

Follow the instructions to write a descriptive paragraph. Use the Writing Checklist to check your work.

Most people wish they had either more time or more money. If you could choose one or the other, which would you choose? Why? Make a list of the ways you would use your extra time or money. On a separate sheet of paper, use your notes to write a detailed paragraph describing the ways the extra time or money would change your lifestyle. Why did you choose that particular option? How would it change your life? How would the people in your life react to the change?

If I could choose either more time or more money, I would choose more money. If I had more money, I would be able to hire a maid. I could pay all of my bills and help out my friends and family with their bills . . .

Writing Checklist

Reflect on your ability to use conditionals by answering the questions.

☐ 1. Did you use real conditionals to talk about possible situations and their results?

☐ 2. Did you use unreal conditional sentences to consider imaginary events and situations?

☐ 3. Did you use any subordinators other than *if*?

☐ 4. Did you omit *if* clauses where possible?

☐ 5. Did you check your sentences for correct form?

14 Noun Clauses

FORM, MEANING, AND USE

1 Examining Form

Read this article and complete the tasks.

A Tale of Two Frank Lloyd Wright Communities

In the late 1940s, several research scientists in Kalamazoo, Michigan decided (that they wanted to create a new residential development). They quickly agreed to hire the famous architect Frank Lloyd Wright, but they had more difficulty choosing <u>where they should build their new community</u>.

By this time, Wright had already designed many of his most famous buildings, such as his Prairie Houses, the Solomon R. Guggenheim Museum, and the masterpiece Fallingwater. During the Great Depression in the 1930s, he had become interested in planning communities and designing affordable houses. He believed that affordable houses should have a style all their own rather than being smaller copies of more expensive homes. He designed houses with a few large rooms instead of many smaller rooms. These houses encouraged more casual living, as they did not contain formal dining rooms or parlors.

The Kalamazoo group liked Wright's philosophy and after contacting him, they found a parcel of land about 10 miles from Kalamazoo. Some of the group members decided that they would like to build the neighborhood there, but others thought that it was too far from the city. They decided to create two separate communities, one in this location and another just outside the city limits. This way the families could choose whether they wanted to live near town or in the country. Wright came to see where his clients wanted their communities, and he was pleased with the land they had chosen. The first community became known as Galesburg Acres and the other became known as Parkwyn Village. Wright designed the site plan for both communities, as well as four of the homes in each community. Thanks to the innovative vision of a group of 1940s professionals, the Kalamazoo area now boasts a unique collection of Frank Lloyd Wright architecture and community planning.

Prairie Houses: Frank Lloyd Wright homes with simple designs and strong horizontal lines
Fallingwater: a Frank Lloyd Wright home built above a waterfall in Bear Run, Pennsylvania
Solomon R. Guggenheim Museum: a modern and contemporary art museum in New York City
Great Depression: a period of widespread poverty in the United Stated during the 1930s

1. Circle four examples of *that* clauses in the article.

2. Underline three examples of *wh-* or *if/whether* clauses in the article.

2 Understanding Time in Sentences with Noun Clauses

Read each sentence. Then choose the correct statement from the box and write it on the line.

> **a.** The noun clause situation occurs before the main clause situation.
>
> **b.** The noun clause situation occurs at the same time as the main clause situation.
>
> **c.** The noun clause situation occurs after the main clause situation.

_a_ 1. I am still wondering why he left the meeting in such a hurry.

_____ 2. All the fans believed their favorite team was going to win the World Series.

_____ 3. Everyone knew that the vice president of the company had taken the money illegally.

_____ 4. It is rumored that a very famous movie star is going to be vacationing in our town!

_____ 5. I wonder why he is lying about today's incident.

_____ 6. I think someone is trying to break into the house!

_____ 7. The family still doesn't know who gave them all those beautiful presents.

_____ 8. They wondered if many people would be able to attend their anniversary party.

3 Introducing Noun Clauses

Complete these conversations by circling the correct word in each set of parentheses. More than one answer may sometimes be possible.

A. Amy: Sam, do you think (why/that/Ø) they'll cancel class tomorrow? They announced (that/what/how)
2   1
there's a lot of ice on the roads.

Sam: I don't know. It's impossible to predict (Ø/whether/that) they'll do that. I never understand
3
(where/Ø/how) they make their decisions.
4

B. Salma: Did you hear (when/that/Ø) the bus is supposed to arrive?
1

Phyllis: Yes, I did. It'll be here by 7:00 this evening. I finally found out (what/whether/that) happened to it,
2
too. It got a flat tire (when/how/Ø) it was leaving the parking lot at the very first stop.
3

4 Writing Sentences Using Noun Clauses

Read the sentences below. Combine each pair of sentences into one sentence. Use *that* clauses and *wh-* or *if/whether* clauses where appropriate.

1. What does he think of the land? The homeowners are wondering about that.
   The homeowners are wondering what the agent thinks of the land.

2. Interest rates were going to rise this year. Everyone believed it.

   _____

3. You should learn to change a tire on your car all by yourself. It is important.

   _____

4. Do her friends like the new house she has chosen to buy? It really doesn't matter.

   _____

5. The family didn't have enough money to pay for Mr. Smith's medical care. That was the problem.

_____

6. What did our boss say in the voicemail message? We should probably listen to it.

_____

7. When are you leaving? I want to leave at that time.

_____

8. The children wanted to leave the beach before the adults did. It was surprising.

_____

5 Using Noun Clauses

Read the information and complete the tasks below.

Home Ownership in Wynfield			
This poll shows how homeowners surveyed in Wynfield answered each of the following questions.			
	YES	**NO**	**NOT SURE**
Do you know what your house is worth?	54%	37%	9%
Do you know if your home has increased in value this year?	34%	59%	7%
Will you buy a new home this year?	12%	61%	27%
Have you decided when you want to retire?	43%	55%	2%
Have you decided where you will retire?	49%	47%	4%
Will you live in your current house after you retire?	48%	21%	31%
Would you suggest that others buy a home in your neighborhood?	43%	18%	39%
Do you know what the crime rate is in your neighborhood?	35%	58%	7%
Do you know who has moved into your neighborhood this year?	74%	23%	3%
Are you satisfied with your current home?	52%	34%	14%

A. Write eight sentences about home ownership in Wynfield. Be sure to use noun clauses and/or infinitives.

1. _43% of homeowners in Wynfield have decided when they want to retire._

2. _____

_____

3. _____

_____

4. _____

_____

5. _____

_____

6. _____

_____

7. _____

_____

8. _____

_____

B. Complete the following sentences using noun clauses to give information regarding your own living situation.

1. The problem is _that housing is very expensive in this city._ .

2. It is important _____ .

3. I wonder _____ .

4. I know _____.

5. I don't know _____.

6. I worry about _____.

7. I don't worry about _____.

8. My friends say _____.

9. It is not necessary _____.

10. It is clear _____.

6 Using Infinitives in Place of Noun Clauses

Rewrite the sentences below so that they contain infinitives instead of noun clauses, when possible. If it isn't possible to change the noun clause to an infinitive, write "Not possible" on the line.

1. They decided that they would build a house in the new neighborhood.
   They decided to build a house in the new neighborhood.

2. I can't decide what I should eat for dinner!
   _____
   _____

3. Frank Lloyd Wright believed that he was designing economical homes for the common man.
   _____
   _____

4. I'm asking that you put my car in the garage so it doesn't get damaged during the storm.
   _____
   _____

5. It is essential that the students arrive on time.
   _____
   _____

6. It absolutely amazes me that Ronald can so easily figure out how to fix electronic devices.
   _____
   _____

7. I was thinking about how I should tell you the news.
   _____
   _____

8. We are having a big debate in our family about when we should take our vacation this year.
   _____
   _____

Find and correct the errors. The first one has been corrected for you.

Dear Lola

Dear Lola,

I have been going out with my boyfriend for three years. The other day he told me ~~what~~ *that* he wants to move to Utah to pursue rock climbing. He says he is going to move whether I went with him or not. I don't want to move to Utah, but I can't imagine my life would be like without him. I don't know why would he want to go without me. Maybe I did something wrong. Do you think I should move to Utah or stay where I am?

— Confused in Chicago

Dear Confused,

I understand it that you really care for your boyfriend, but I don't think whether he is serious about your relationship. You may wonder why he wants to move, but it's not worth the trouble. Please don't waste time trying to figure it out what you did wrong. This is his decision and it's not your fault. I suggest that you are staying where you feel more comfortable there.

Follow the instructions to write two paragraphs about a change you would like someone that you know to make. Use the Writing Checklist to check your work.

In the first paragraph, write about the reason you want to see this change happen. Who is the person and how do you know him/her? What is the problem as you see it? What does this person think about the problem? How does the problem affect this person's life? Does this problem affect others? In the second paragraph, write about the change you recommend. What is the change this person should make? How would this change make the situation better? How would the change affect you? Who else would it affect? Why is making this change important?

My brother, Archie, is constantly late for work. He leaves home when he should already be at work. His boss has told him that he will fire him if he doesn't start showing up on time. I'm afraid he'll lose his job and won't be able to pay his bills . . .

Writing Checklist

Reflect on your ability to use noun clauses by answering the questions.

- ☐ 1. Did you use *that* clauses to explain your thoughts and feeling about something?
- ☐ 2. Did you use any *that* clauses after expressions of necessity or advice?
- ☐ 3. Did you link *wh-* clauses with *that* clauses to introduce explanations?
- ☐ 4. Did you use *wh-* clauses and *if/whether* clauses to talk about a question that you want to answer?
- ☐ 5. Did you use *that* clauses with *it* subjects + passive verbs?
- ☐ 6. Did you check your sentences for correct form?

15 Reported Speech

FORM, MEANING, AND USE

1 **Examining Form**

Read this newspaper article and complete the tasks.

To Serve and Protect

Captain Marcus Johnson of the Maysville Police Department will be retiring this fall after 35 years on the job. According to Mayor Rivera, "the captain has done more than his share to combat crime in the greater Maysville area." I had a chance to sit down with Captain Johnson and ask him about his distinguished career. When asked what the best part of his career was, the captain smiled and said he enjoyed meeting so many wonderful people along the way. He explained that he felt fulfilled every time he had a chance to help a youngster avoid a life of crime. He also stated that his coworkers made every day of work a pleasure. "When you're part of such a dynamic team, you can't go wrong," he said. Of course, fighting crime in our city can't always be a walk in the park. When asked about the most frustrating aspect of his job, Captain Johnson answered that it was the dishonesty. He said it was very disappointing to see how many people would lie for any reason at all. The captain claimed that people could be happier if they learned to tell the truth. He told me that people would lie to get out of a traffic tickets, to hide the crimes of others, or to get themselves out of trouble. He added that the most disturbing cases were those in which a person would lie for no reason at all. "All those lies sure did make it difficult to get the job done." Luckily for Maysville, Captain Johnson did get the job done during his long career. Let's hope his replacement can live up to his standards.

---

distinguished: successful and respected
fulfilled: satisfied; having met with the desired results
youngster: a young person

dynamic: energized and enthusiastic
a walk in the park: easy, leisurely
aspect: part, element

1. An example of quoted speech in the article is circled. Find two more and circle brackets around them.

2. Underline six examples of reported speech.

3. Look at the following sentence: "The captain claimed that people could be happier if they learned to tell the truth." Why doesn't the verb in the noun clause change form?

   _____ a. The captain is talking about a future event.

   _____ b. The captain is using a modal of advisability or possibility.

Choose the correct response to each statement or question. There may be more than one correct answer for each.

1. "I asked him how old he was." The speaker . . .
   a. is asking a question.
   b. is reporting what he said.
   c. wanted to know someone's age.
   d. is asking someone to do something.

2. "Sara told him that she doesn't want the job." The speaker . . .
   a. offered Sara a job.
   b. is reporting what Sara said to someone else.
   c. is reporting a future event.
   d. is talking about something that was said in the past.

3. "Andrea said her friends are visiting from Buenos Aires." The verb form in the noun clause has not been changed because it is . . .
   a. a current situation.
   b. a timeless statement.
   c. a habitual activity.
   d. a future event.

4. "I have to leave at 10:00, even if the meeting isn't finished yet." The speaker . . .
   a. is asking if it is okay for her to leave at 10:00.
   b. is talking about a future event.
   c. is admitting that she made a mistake.
   d. insists that she must leave at 10:00.

5. "My friends all asked me how I made the cookies." The speaker's friends . . .
   a. promised to make her some cookies.
   b. wanted to know how to make the cookies.
   c. requested her recipe for cookies.
   d. asked someone else for the recipe.

6. "Dan told me I had won a prize." Dan . . .
   a. gave the speaker some news.
   b. won a prize.
   c. made a general announcement.
   d. was speaking about a habitual activity.

7. "My teacher suggested that I buy a dictionary." The speaker . . .
   a. is repeating some advice his teacher gave him.
   b. has definitely bought a dictionary.
   c. is talking about an announcement the teacher made to the class.
   d. is repeating a question his teacher asked him.

8. "I told her that I used to study until 11:00 every night." The speaker . . .
   a. still studies until 11:00 every night.
   b. is describing a habitual activity in the past.
   c. is talking about something he did.
   d. is describing something that just happened.

3 Understanding Reported Speech

Match each quote with an accurate example of reported speech.

1. I will be having dinner with the committee on Tuesday. __E__

2. I have dinner with the committee on Tuesdays. _____

3. I have to have dinner with the committee on Tuesday. _____

4. I could have dinner with the committee on Tuesday. _____

5. Where will I have dinner with the committee on Tuesday? _____

6. I had dinner with the committee last Tuesday. _____

a. He said he had dinner with the committee on Tuesday.

b. He wants to know where he will have dinner with the committee on Tuesday.

c. He said he has dinner with the committee every Tuesday.

d. He said he would be able to have dinner with the committee on Tuesday.

e. He said he would be having dinner with the committee on Tuesday.

f. He said he had to have dinner with the committee on Tuesday.

4 Writing Direct Speech

Read the sentences below. Rewrite what the people said in direct speech. Change tenses and pronouns where appropriate.

1. They asked why I hadn't bought a new car yet.
   "Why haven't you bought a new car yet?" _____

2. Alfredo told me he'd help me with my homework.
   _____
   _____

3. My roommate insisted that I help him clean the house.
   _____
   _____

4. He admitted that he cheated on the exam.
   _____
   _____

5. Nicole said she'd fix the car later.
   _____
   _____

6. The instructor said the students used to turn in plagiarized papers.
   _____
   _____

7. My lawyer told me I should tell the truth.
   _____
   _____

8. The teacher wanted to know how long we studied for the exam.
   _____
   _____

5 Contrasting Reporting Verbs

Choose the best word to complete each sentence.

1. I (told/suggested/inquired) that she finish her homework before the party.

2. Everyone came (to tell/to ask/to inquire) me how I was feeling.

3. Maria (insisted/told/said) that everyone help her rehearse her lines for the play.

4. My colleagues have (assured/asked/said) us that it won't be a problem.

5. You (asked/insisted/promised) to help us with this project!

6. Mr. Johnson (advised/demanded/questioned) us to plan ahead.

7. We (said/told/asked) our family the good news.

8. Steve (told/proposed/said) he's really tired tonight.

9. Mrs. Reynolds is (requesting/saying/asking) extra help with the report.

10. Jan (asked/insisted/demanded) why we weren't at the meeting.

6 Using Reported Speech

Read this conversation and complete the task below.

1. **Vera:** Hey, can you come to a meeting in my office later?

2. **Paco:** Probably not. I'm really busy.

3. **Vera:** Why are you so busy?

4. **Paco:** I'm working on the budget.

5. **Vera:** But you have to come! I insist!

6. **Paco:** Why do you want me there?

7. **Vera:** I want to discuss expanding the department and I need your support.

8. **Paco:** What time is the meeting?

9. **Vera:** It's at 3:30 this afternoon.

10. **Paco:** Okay, I'll be there. I promise!

Paraphrase each of the sentences in the dialogue in order to report what was said.

1. _Vera asked Paco if he could come to the meeting today._

2. _____

3. _____

4. _____

5. _____

6. _____

7. _____

8. _____

9. _____

10. _____

Choose the best word to complete each sentence.

1. "Will you stay after work to help?"

   She asked if (she/I/my) would stay after work to help.

2. "Have you seen my keys?"

   He asked if I had seen (my/their/his) keys.

3. "I'm going to have dinner with him tonight."

   She said she's going to have dinner with (he/him/me) tonight.

4. "We always stop at Exit 14 for coffee."

   They said (we/they/you) always stop at Exit 14 for coffee.

5. "I'm sorry, but I broke your lamp."

   He admitted that he broke (your/my/his) lamp.

6. We can't go out to dinner looking like this!

   She said (we/you/I) can't go out to dinner looking like this.

8 **Editing**

Find and correct the errors. The first one has been corrected for you.

A Different Kind of Spring Break

Today I interviewed a group of college students who spent their spring break exploring an ice age cave in Missouri that was accidentally found by construction workers several years back. The students ~~told~~ *said* that they had sign up for this ten-day experience for a number of different reasons. Some said me that they were looking for something different to do besides partying during spring break. A few mentioned that we had read about the famous cave in the newspaper and wanted to learn more about it for ourselves. Others wanted to find out if paleontology was an interesting major? No matter what their reasons, the students reported what they certainly were not disappointed.

In fact, their team leader said they even make some important discoveries in the cave. She explained that the group had found a large number of microfossils dating back almost a million years and they also find some tracks in the clay, presumably of large cats. She informed that these findings and others have raised a number of interesting questions for further research. For example, experts were wondering does the claw print in the cave belong to the largest bear species ever to walk the earth.

Follow the instructions to write a paragraph about a disagreement or argument you had in the past year. Use the Writing Checklist to check your work.

Think about a disagreement or argument you had within the past year. Make a few notes. Who did you disagree with? How many people were involved? What was the disagreement about? What advice did others give you about it? How did you resolve it? On a separate sheet of paper, use your notes to write a detailed paragraph describing the dispute. Use direct speech and reported speech as appropriate.

The other day, I had an argument with my brother. He said that I hadn't told him about the dinner I was planning for our parents. I told him that I actually remember the day I mentioned the event to him . . .

Writing Checklist

Reflect on your ability to use reported speech by answering the questions.

☐ 1. Did you use any examples of past tense reporting?

☐ 2. Did you choose not to change the verb in any reported language to keep the meaning clear?

☐ 3. Did you use any examples of present tense reporting or the reported imperative?

☐ 4. Did you paraphrase reported speech to make it more concise?

☐ 5. Did you use a combination of quoted speech, reported speech, and alternatives to reported speech?

☐ 6. Did you check your sentences for correct form?

Chapters 13–15

A. Choose the most appropriate response.

1. If you hadn't told everyone I was going to resign, no one would know!
   a. Yes, but I did.
   b. But I'm not going to tell them.

2. I always like to explore the cities when I go on vacation.
   a. I didn't. I preferred the beach.
   b. So do I.

3. So you got to the theatre after the play had started.
   a. Yes. I wouldn't have been late if there hadn't been traffic.
   b. Yes. I wouldn't be late if there wasn't traffic.

4. We could go to the movies tonight if we weren't babysitting.
   a. Great idea! Let's do that.
   b. I know. It's a shame.

5. Will the flight be delayed?
   a. Yes, as long as the weather is bad.
   b. Yes, unless the weather is bad.

6. If you have time, could you help me with this problem?
   a. I'm sorry, I won't have time.
   b. I'm sorry I didn't have time.

B. Complete the sentences. More than one answer may be possible in some cases.

7. If Pete didn't say hello, it's probably because he _____ remember you.

8. I might go swimming if it _____ too cold.

9. Whenever I _____ the dog for a walk, he chases a rabbit.

10. Unless you want to make yourself unpopular, I really _____ say that.

11. If you enjoyed *Love Actually*, you _____ like Hugh Grant's latest film, too.

12. I can't understand why you act _____ if you knew all the answers.

13. If the school had more money, it _____ definitely run evening classes.

14. I'd retire if I _____ you.

C. Combine each pair of sentences to form a noun clause with *that,* a *wh-* word, or *if/whether.* More than one answer may be possible.

15. What did the announcer say? I couldn't hear him.

   _____

16. Can I tell you who the new boss is? I don't know.

   _____

17. We don't have enough time. It's a problem.

   _____

18. Where did you go last night? I want to hear all about it.

   _____

19. Does he love me? I'm not sure.

   _____

20. Grandma is still skydiving at 90. It's almost embarrassing.

   _____

D. Find the incorrectly reported sentences and correct them. If a sentence is correct, put a check (✓).

21. "I'm a professional clown."

   _____ He said me he was a professional clown.

22. "Would you pick up my dry-cleaning?'

   _____ She asked me if I would pick up my dry-cleaning.

23. "I called you yesterday"

   _____ He insisted that he'd called me the next day.

24. "Are you feeling better?"

   _____ He wanted to know was I feeling better.

25. "I'm 59."

   _____ She says she's 59.

26. "The polar caps are going to melt."

   _____ Experts warned us that the polar caps were melting.

27. So, when do you start your new job?

   _____ He wanted to know when I had started my new job.

28. "I'm not going to enjoy tomorrow's meeting."

   _____ She said she wasn't going to enjoy the meeting the following day.

29. "Don't worry."

   _____ He told don't worry.

30. "I hadn't seen him before."

   _____ She claimed she didn't see him before.

Workbook Answer Key

CHAPTER 1   THE PRESENT

Exercise 1 (p. 4)

The use of the Spanish language in the United States <u>is growing</u> rapidly, and its influence <u>is</u> evident throughout the country. The widespread use of Spanish (is) no longer limited to New York, Florida, Texas, and California. In recent years, the use of Spanish <u>has been spreading</u> further into the interior of the country. Spanish <u>has become</u> important in states such as Utah, Michigan, and North Carolina, for example. In an effort to appeal to all of these Spanish speakers, companies (are advertising) in Spanish throughout the country, both on television and in print. Businesses of all kinds (are striving) to hire bilingual staff members to communicate with their Hispanic clients. Professionals in nearly every field (are signing up) for Spanish classes in order to expand their opportunities and earn more money.

Spanish (has) definitely (changed) life in the United States, but it (is) also clear that Spanish itself (has been changing) because of its close contact with English. Consider, for example, the many large bilingual communities that (have been thriving) all over the country. Because of the relationship between English and Spanish in these communities, many Spanish speakers (have created) Spanish words that come from English. For example, the word for "to have lunch" in Spanish (is) "almorzar," but many Spanish speakers in the U.S. (prefer) to use the word "lonchear." The traditional way to say "to park (the car)" in Spanish (is) "estacionar (el carro)," although in Miami you (are) more likely to hear the phrase "parquear (el carro)." This (is) an interesting time for the Spanish language in the United States. No one really (knows) what changes lie ahead for both the language and the country.

2. a. This action is ongoing.

Exercise 2 (p. 5)

2. c	4. a	6. a, c	8. b
3. c	5. b	7. a, c	

Exercise 3 (p. 6)

2. Celia works further from home.
3. Marc has already driven to work and checked his e-mail.
4. Celia is preparing budget reports.
5. Celia has been preparing budget reports since 8:30 A.M./ for an hour.
6. Marc is answering client e-mails.
7. Marc spends more time with clients
8. It is 12 P.M.
9. Marc and Celia are eating dinner.
10. They've been eating dinner since 6:15 P.M./for fifteen minutes.

Exercise 4 (p. 6)

A.
2. says/has been saying
3. am/'ve been
4. watch
5. scare

B.
1. are
2. 'm writing
3. is
4. 've been working

C.
1. 'm having/'ve been having
2. want
3. 've traveled
4. know
5. 've studied/'ve been studying
6. think

Exercise 5 (p. 7)

2. a	4. c	6. c
3. a, b	5. a	

Exercise 6 (p. 7)

1. d	3. b	5. c
2. f	4. a	6. e

Exercise 7 (p. 8)

Are you interested in learning a second language? _Have_ ~~Has~~ you been frustrated at your slow progress so far? Well, Super Speaker software is for you! Millions of students have tried our language learning software and they have _not been_ ~~been not~~ disappointed. In conjunction with classroom learning, our software has _helped_ ~~helping~~ students around the country learn a second language very quickly. Take Stephanie, for example. With our free demo, she _has reported_ ~~reports~~ that she has ~~been~~ learned Korean twice as fast! Our programs ✗ _are_ available to learners of English, Spanish, French, Korean, Japanese, and Chinese. Another user, Ken, is a very busy man. He works full time, attends classes, and _helps_ ~~helping~~ his mother take care of her house. He says our program has been a lifesaver! Similarly, Sasha is studying English, _taking_ ~~takes~~ care of her children, and is looking for a job in the United States. Our program helps her focus on all her goals at once. She _knows_ ~~know~~ she will find a job now that her English is improving so quickly. All of these customers have ~~noticing~~ _noticed_ a big difference in their language learning with Super Speaker software. They ∧_have_ not been this satisfied with any other product. What you are waiting for? Order your free demo today!

Exercise 8 (p. 8)

Answers will vary.

CHAPTER 2   THE PAST

Exercise 1 (p. 9)

Bob was eating (dinner when) it happened. He and his wife were talking (about the w)eekend and the anchorman was reading (the news on) TV. At first, Bob and his wife weren't paying attention (to the TV,) but at 7:00 they <u>tuned</u> in to see the winning lottery n(umbers. Bob) was thinking about what he would do with the eight million dollar jackpot, but he <u>didn't</u> really <u>think</u> he would win. The television reporter <u>read</u> the winning numbers and Bob heard his wife scream. He <u>read</u> the numbers on the TV screen, but he <u>didn't</u> <u>believe</u> what he saw. It couldn't be true! The winning lottery numbers he <u>saw</u> on the TV were the same numbers on the ticket in his wife's hand. Many thoughts (were racing) through Bob's mind. He <u>knew</u> his life would never be the same again.

Bob was right. His life <u>changed</u> that day. The day before, he and his wife [had been living] a normal life, but the lottery <u>made</u> them famous. Right away, Bob's friends (were asking) for money. Old acquaintances (were calling) him "just to catch up on old times." They <u>pretended</u> to be surprised when Bob told them about the lottery. He and his wife <u>received</u> many visitors, but they <u>felt</u> isolated from the world. Finally, they <u>decided</u> to move to a small island in the Caribbean, where nobody <u>knew</u> about the lottery. That is how Bob <u>began</u> the biggest adventure of his life.

3. b

Exercise 2 (p. 10)

A. 2. a   4. b   6. b
    3. a   5. a
B. 1. a
    2. b

Exercise 3 (p. 10)

Answers will vary. Some examples are:
2. Have you ever lived in another country?
   No, I haven't.
3. Has he ever met anyone famous?
   Yes, he has.
4. Have you ever had an unusual job?
   No, I haven't.
5. Has she ever run a marathon?
   Yes, she has.
6. Have you ever regretted telling the truth?
   No, I haven't.
7. Have you ever had an accident?
   Yes, I have.
8. Have they ever eaten catfish?
   No, they haven't.

Exercise 4 (p. 11)

2. was
3. was shining
4. was walking/walked
5. ran
6. had seen
7. was
8. was barking
9. didn't see
10. got
11. called
12. came
13. ran
14. chased
15. happened
16. caught up
17. didn't bite
18. lay down
19. rolled

Exercise 5 (p. 11)

Answers will vary. Some examples are:
Mario: Wow! That's early. What <u>did</u> you <u>do</u> next?
Ana: <u>I had coffee and some social time.</u>
Mario: Oh, I see. I called you at 1:00 P.M., but you didn't answer. What <u>were</u> you <u>doing</u>?
Ana: <u>I was having lunch with the marketing department.</u>
Mario: <u>Had</u> you already <u>heard</u> President Smith's speech by that time?
Ana: <u>Yes, I had.</u>
Mario: Oh, that's nice. What <u>happened</u> after lunch?
Ana: <u>I had computer training.</u>
Mario: Oh, good. Working with computers can be tricky. <u>Did</u> you <u>get</u> a tour of the company buildings?
Ana: <u>Yes, I got a tour at 3:15 P.M.</u>
Mario: I'll bet that was interesting. You know, I thought you <u>finished</u> work at 5:00pm, so I called you at 5:05 P.M. <u>Were</u> you still <u>working</u>?
Ana: <u>I was having a meeting with my immediate supervisor.</u>
Mario: Really? That sounds like a long day. What time <u>did</u> you <u>leave</u> work?
Ana: <u>I left work at 5:15 P.M.</u>

Exercise 6 (p. 12)

2. a   4. b   6. c
3. b   5. a

Exercise 7 (p. 13)

This year's Spring Fashion Show was the best ever. At 10:00 A.M., the models ~~was~~ _were_ arriving and the photographers were taking pictures. The fans ~~has~~ _had_ been waiting in the streets for several hours. Everyone was ~~cheered~~ _cheering_ when the famous designers ~~walking~~ _were walking_ down the red carpet. All the spectators had taken their seats inside the theater when the show began. The models ~~walk~~ _walked_ down the runway in the season's most beautiful new fashions. Each model walked to the end of the runway and turned slowly so everyone could see the fashions clearly. The photographers ~~was~~ _were_ snapping pictures and the crowd ~~were~~ _was_ cheering enthusiastically throughout the entire show. The most popular designs of the season ~~including~~ _included_ bright colors and straight lines. Most of the designs ~~been~~ featured long flowing skirts and suits. The shirts ~~was~~ _were_ loose with long

sleeves. They are the best creations the fashion world has
ever ~~seeing~~ *seen*.

Exercise 8 (p. 13)

Answers will vary.

CHAPTER 3   THE FUTURE

Exercise 1 (p. 14)

If you choose to join us, your trip (will begin) with a
one night stay in Miami. <u>Your cruise leaves Miami at 6:00
A.M. on March 3 and remains at sea for six nights and
seven days.</u> While at sea, you (will experience) the finest
food, entertainment, and lodging the Caribbean has
to offer. Your stateroom (will have) an ocean view and a
private bathroom. Prepare to feast on succulent food each
evening in our Sunset Dining Room, where you (will dine)
on the freshest fish and seafood. All passengers (will enjoy)
our indoor pool and our three outdoor pools.

You <u>are going to love</u> our fitness programs. We offer
water aerobics, spinning, and yoga classes. Join us for
organized sporting events such as water volleyball. The
Sunrise Deck hosts activities such as shuffleboard, mini
golf, and jogging. Perhaps you<u>'ll have had</u> enough sun by
the end of the day. In that case, you(<u>'ll head</u>) inside to watch
our premiere live entertainment. You (will) also (be able to)
take dancing lessons, go bowling, or enjoy our bars and
dance clubs. Sound like fun? Well, after doing all this you
still <u>won't have left</u> the ship! But by the end of your cruise,
you <u>will have visited</u> beautiful Puerto Rico, the fabulous
Bahamas, and the ever popular Grand Cayman Island. You
(won't find) a vacation like this anywhere else, so join us for
our cruise in the sunny Caribbean!

3. b

Exercise 2 (p. 15)

2. a	4. a, b, c	6. a, c	8. a, b, c
3. a, b	5. a	7. a	

Exercise 3 (p. 15)

A. 1. b   3. d   5. a
       2. e   4. c   6. f

B. Answers will vary.

Exercise 4 (p. 16)

B. a. 2, 7; Sentence 7 is more definite.
       b. 1, 10
       c. 3, 9
       d. 4, 6
       e. 5, 8

Exercise 5 (p. 16)

1. f   3. b   5. e
2. a   4. c   6. d

Exercise 6 (p. 16)

2. will have gotten her boarding pass
3. will have checked her baggage
4. will have left
5. will have arrived
6. will have been traveling

Exercise 7 (p. 17)

2. S
3. D
   We're going to be happy if this business is a success.
4. S
5. D
   Jake is going to help us with the projects.
6. S

Exercise 8 (p. 18)

Our town has a reputation for preserving our historic
buildings. Thanks to the efforts of concerned citizens,
our grandchildren will ~~enjoying~~ *enjoy* Main Street's historic
storefronts and many other important landmarks. In the
past thirty years, our citizens have worked hard to save
our history for future generations One of our lesser-known
historic buildings is currently being threatened, however,
by new development. If citizens do not act, we ~~will~~ *are*
going to lose a very important building in our city's
landscape. A company called Knox Developing is going to
~~have~~ purchase the Morton Building with plans to knock
it down. The Morton Building will ~~has~~ *have* vanished within a
few months unless we can stop the purchase. According
to Marty Rogers, Smithfield Historic Preservation Council
chairman, the council ~~are~~ *is* going to try and have the
building added to the National Register of Historic Places.
"We ~~is~~ *are* going to speak to the judge and request~~ed~~ a court
order to halt demolition of the building. We ~~are~~ *are going to/will*
organize
large groups of concerned citizens to protest when Knox
Developing ~~will arrive~~ *arrives* at the site. We will let the developer
know that the demolition of historic buildings will ~~be not~~ *not be*
acceptable in Smithfield," said Rogers.

Exercise 9 (p. 18)

Answers will vary.

CHAPTER 4   MODALS

Exercise 1 (p. 21)

Many professionals in the field of psychology believe
that astrology is outdated and irrelevant in today's world.
They say people (shouldn't follow) the advice they read in
their horoscopes. These professionals say that people
(must use) astrology as a form of entertainment only. They
fear that patients (might take) astrology too seriously and
make bad decisions.

Clinical psychologist Gary L. Burke, PhD, disagrees
with these professionals, however. Dr. Burke says
astrology is an ancient science that (should be) included in

the practice of modern psychology. While he agrees that patients (must not rely) on astrology alone, he believes professional interpretation of a patient's astrological chart at birth (may help) the patient and psychologist gain a better understanding of a patient's thought process.

Dr. Burke admits that there are many fraudulent astrology websites and businesses that offer people vague and useless information. He says patients (shouldn't) always (follow) the advice they read in a newspaper horoscope. "Many people make claims to be astrologists when they are really just writers looking to make some easy money. The public (should not associate) these people with the real science of professional astrology. There are many professional astrologists who offer high-quality, in-depth readings, however. We (could combine) their work with modern psychology to offer the best possible service to the modern public," says Dr. Burke.

2. a. T
   b. F

Exercise 2 (p. 22)

1. 2, 6   4. 3, 8
   a. 6   a. 3
   b. 2   b. 8
2. 1, 10   5. 4, 5
   a. 10   a. 4
   b. 1   b. 5
3. 7, 9
   a. 9
   b. 7

Exercise 3 (p. 22)

Answers will vary. Some examples are:
2. John shouldn't have believed his horoscope.
3. John shouldn't have told his wife that she was a bad cook.
4. John had better find a new job.
1. Katya shouldn't have eaten shrimp.
2. Katya should have told her friends that she was allergic to shrimp.
3. Katya had better go to the hospital.
4. Katya ought to have made an excuse.

Exercise 4 (p. 23)

2. b, d   4. b, c   6. c, d   8. a, b
3. b, c   5. a, b   7. d

Exercise 5 (p. 24)

1. shouldn't have   6. had better
2. may be   7. ought to
3. must   8. doesn't have to
4. might have   9. couldn't
5. may not   10. might not

Exercise 6 (p. 24)

2. must not have   5. doesn't have to work
   remembered   6. was supposed to work
3. might have been   7. should ask
4. may have happened   8. must be

Exercise 7 (p. 25)

ARIES (March 21-April 20): You should ~~been~~ *be* walking on air right now! The stars are in line and you just may ~~getting~~ *be getting* everything your heart desires this month.

TAURUS (April 21 – May 20): Wake up! You should ~~to~~ be out socializing more. You have been unhappy, but your social life could be more exciting this month.

GEMINI (May 21 – June 20): You had ~~not better~~ *better not* spend all your money this month. Mars is urging you to splurge, so you must be careful to make good decisions.

CANCER (June 21 – July 21): You could have problems with your partner this month. Work hard to keep the peace even when your sweetie is being less than sweet.

LEO (July 22 – August 21): You couldn't be happier! You should have great luck in love and at work this month. You may even get that proposal you've wanted.

VIRGO (August 22 – September 21): Don't look now, but you could be in trouble. You ~~should~~ *shouldn't* have been so careless last month.

LIBRA (September 22 – October 21): This month should be life-changing for you. You will finally be excited about that big change on the horizon.

SCORPIO (October 22 – November 21): You could ~~has~~ *have* worked harder last month. Now you must ~~working~~ *work* hard to make up for all the fun you had then!

SAGITTARIUS (November 22 – December 20): You'd better not ~~made~~ *make* any big decisions this month. Venus is in the area to cause problems and confusion.

CAPRICORN (December 21 – January 19): You don't ~~has~~ *have* to solve that problem this month, but you will feel a lot better if you do. You may even get more money.

AQUARIUS (January 20 – February 18): You might not ~~seeing~~ *be seeing* great results this month, but everything you do should lead to prosperity in the future.

PISCES (February 19 – March 20): You should see big changes at work this month. You may ~~wanted~~ *want* to be on the lookout for a big announcement.

Exercise 8 (p. 26)

Answers will vary.

CHAPTER 5   THE PASSIVE

Exercise 1 (p. 27)

Every year, millions of students apply to enter colleges and universities in the United States. Many of these students (are required to take) standardized college entrance exams. Their exam scores (can be sent) directly to the colleges of their choice. The exams are very difficult and last for many hours. The students must pay a fee and arrive at the testing site early in the morning. Some of the exams test general aptitude, while others test subjects that students (are expected) to learn in high school, including mathematics, science, and English. The questions (are chosen) by a group of educators and researchers.

Colleges and universities use the exam scores, along with an applicant's high school grades to determine whether the applicant (will be admitted). A college or university may also consider a student's extracurricular activities and work history when making decisions about admission.

Some people feel that colleges and universities pay too much attention to these exam scores. They feel other factors, such as high school grades and extracurricular activities, (should be considered) more carefully. Other people believe the tests are a fair and accurate way to predict how successful the student will be in college. They say high school grades (are assigned) differently by each teacher, but standardized tests are the same for everyone. No matter what people say about standardized college entrance exams, they (are likely to be used) in the United States for many years to come.

2. Answers will vary. Some examples are:
Universities require many of these students to take standardized college entrance exams.
Colleges and universities use the exam scores, along with an applicant's high school grades, to determine whether to admit the applicant.

Exercise 2 (p. 28)

2. a, b, c   4. a, b, c   6. a
3. b   5. c

Exercise 3 (p. 28)

A. 2. Akiko ironed the clothes.
   3. The floor was swept by Ashley.
   4. The trash was taken out by Danielle.
   5. The bathroom was cleaned by Heather.
   6. Jasette washed the clothes.
B. 2. Ashley swept the floor.
   3. Danielle took out the trash.
   4. Heather cleaned the bathroom.

Exercise 4 (p. 29)

2. by a graduate teaching assistant
3. by high-tech machines
4. by the anatomy students
5. by hurricane-force winds
6. by three hundred thousand visitors

Exercise 5 (p. 29)

2. a   4. b   6. a
3. b   5. b

Exercise 6 (p. 29)

2. My window was broken by your children!
3. X
4. A lot of rice is eaten in Japan.
5. A fund-raising event is going to be held next week.
6. Proper grammar should be taught in high schools.
7. Exam preparation courses should be taken by every student.
8. X
9. Traffic was stopped at the intersection.
10. The lecture is being given by a guest speaker.
11. X
12. My husband's wallet was stolen yesterday.

Exercise 7 (p. 30)

1. collided   5. are being told
2. were damaged   6. have been caused
3. was hurt   7. saw
4. are gathering

Exercise 8 (p. 30)

Morris: Good evening, Rebecca. Thank you for taking time to speak with us. I want you to know that this interview is being seen by our viewers at home. Where were you when the accident occurred?

Rebecca: Good evening, Morris. I was standing right here on this corner. That yellow car was hit by the blue car as it was going through the intersection.

Morris: Was anyone hurt?

Rebecca: Well, I'm no doctor, but I'd say the driver of the blue car was injured pretty badly.

Morris: How do you know that?

Rebecca: Well, as he was being pulled out of the car by the paramedics, he was yelling about his right arm. One of the paramedics said it may have been broken.

Morris: And what about the passengers and the driver of the yellow car?

Rebecca: I didn't see any passengers. The driver of the yellow car was taken to the hospital as a precaution, but he told the paramedics that he felt fine.

Morris: Well, that's good news. Were you hit by any flying debris from the crash?

Rebecca: No, I wasn't.

Exercise 9 (p. 31)

Answers will vary.

CHAPTER 6   NOUNS AND NOUN MODIFIERS

Exercise 1 (p. 32)

My best friend had to go to (Costa Rica) for business this summer. After studying some tourist <u>information</u>, I decided to go with her and spend some extra <u>time</u> touring the country. (Costa Rica) is not very far from the (United States), but we had to take three separate flights to get to our first destination, (Playa Samara). (Playa Samara) is a small beach town located in the (Guanacaste) peninsula. It has one of the most beautiful beaches in the world, and the town is rustic and friendly. We stayed in a tiny inn right on the beach. The <u>water</u> was magnificent and we enjoyed at least an hour of <u>swimming</u> every day.

After leaving (Playa Samara), we toured many other famous areas in the country, including the (Arenal Volcano), the (Monteverde Cloud Forest), and the (Tortuguero) area on the (Caribbean) coast. I had never been outside the (United States) before and I was really excited to see what life is like in (Central America). The <u>weather</u> was very hot near the beach, but it was much cooler in the center of the country, where the elevation is higher. Summer is the rainy season in (Costa Rica), so there was a rain shower almost every afternoon. The <u>food</u> was wonderful. We ate <u>rice</u> and <u>chicken</u> every day and almost always had a piece of tropical <u>fruit</u> with our breakfast. In (San Jose), the capital, I did a lot of <u>shopping</u> while my friend researched business opportunities. She owns a business called (Exotic Furniture) that imports <u>furniture</u> to the (United States), and she made some business contacts in (Costa Rica). I hope she works with them often, because I want to visit the country again soon.

Exercise 2 (p. 32)

2. a	4. a, b, c	6. c	8. a
3. b, c	5. a, b	7. a, c	

Exercise 3 (p. 33)

2. They saw some ancient Roman pottery.
3. I bought a small black reading lamp.
4. It was in a beautiful old theater.
5. Lindsey is wearing the brown and pink sweater.
6. I want a rectangular wooden table.

Exercise 4 (p. 34)

1. chocolate-covered	4. long-running
2. five-mile	5. Cuban-made
3. mean-spirited	6. high-calorie

Exercise 5 (p. 34)

2. N	4. C	6. N	8. C
3. N	5. N	7. N	

Exercise 6 (p. 34)

2. is deciding	9. belongs
3. is	10. is
4. is	11. was
5. were playing	12. wants
6. has	13. are required
7. are being invested	14. seems
8. is	

Exercise 7 (p. 35)

A.

2. in		7. of
3. to		8. of
4. of		9. of
5. for		10. with
6. to		

B. 4, 7, 9

Exercise 8 (p. 35)

A.

2. scuba diving	4. credit card
3. coral reef	5. exit door

B.

1. dishwasher	4. floor lamps
2. washing machine	5. table lamps
3. clothes drier	6. house guests

Exercise 9 (p. 36)

I am responding to the opinion column written by Frank in Newtonville. My opinion and his opinion ~~is~~ *are* very different. Frank doesn't believe that American-~~own~~ *owned* companies should have any involvement ~~to~~ *with/in* international firms. Frank is afraid there will be many problems with the economy if we invest in Central American countries. Well, there ~~is~~ *are* many problems with the economy right now, and we are solving ~~it~~ *them* by investing in Central American countries. I belong to a three-year~~s~~-old international business group. Our group ~~are~~ *is* working every day to improve the ~~economy~~ *economies* in the United States and other countries. Research~~es~~ shows that by working together, we can achieve great results. Cooperation and understanding ~~is~~ *are* our greatest tools at this time.

Exercise 10 (p. 36)

Answers will vary.

CHAPTER 7   ARTICLES AND OTHER DETERMINERS

Exercise 1 (p. 39)

Some of you have already met Professor Chiara Busseni, a visiting professor of art history. She arrived in (New York City) in August and will be teaching at our university for two years. She comes from Italy and is an expert in Renaissance sculpture. I recently had a chance meet Professor Busseni and hear her impressions of life in our city. "<u>New York City</u> is so alive and vibrant," she said. "There is so much diversity in <u>the city</u>, which is exciting. <u>It</u> can seem big and overwhelming at first, but I already feel at home here." (Professor Busseni) said every Sunday <u>she</u> enjoys eating a traditional American breakfast at a diner near her apartment. She sometimes visits the Little Italy neighborhood when she wants to hear her native language or buy Italian items. Most of the time, though, she chooses to try new things. She loves New York City's wide variety of foods and other goods from around the world. She also relishes visiting a different museum every weekend, such as the Guggenheim.

When I asked Professor Busseni to tell me her favorite place in the city, she enthusiastically said, "Oh, (Central Park) is the best! I love going to the park on a warm afternoon when I can eat an ice cream cone and read. I even grade my students' papers there. It's a very relaxing place." So what is her least favorite part of the city? "The traffic!" she says. "But I'm getting used to it." It seems as though New York City has made a great impression on Professor Busseni. Let's give her a warm welcome to our university.

1. Central Park, the park, It
2.   a.   the Guggenheim
     b.   her
     c.   a diner
     d.   the traffic

Exercise 2 (p. 40)

2. b   4. a, b, c   6. a, b, c
3. a, b   5. a

Exercise 3 (p. 40)

A. 2. Ø   5. the   8. Ø
    3. the   6. a   9. a
    4. Ø   7. the/Ø
B. 1. the   4. the   7. a
    2. an   5. an
    3. Ø   6. Ø

Exercise 4 (p. 41)

A. 2. That   4. those
    3. that   5. this
B. 1. this   3. this
    2. those   4. those

Exercise 5 (p. 41)

1. e   3. a   5. c
2. d   4. b   6. f

Exercise 6 (p. 42)

1. The poster is advertising an outdoor summer concert.
2. The event begins at 6:30 P.M..
3. You should bring nonperishable food items.
4. The event will take place at the Municipal Park Bandshell.
5. An accomplished guitarist will perform.
6. The event is taking place to benefit The City Shelter.
7. Answers will vary.
8. Answers will vary.

Exercise 7 (p. 42)

2. d, a steak   5. a, a movie
3. f, the bank   6. b, the president.
4. c, the ones

Exercise 8 (p. 43)

Living in *a* big city has many advantages and disadvantages. It is sometimes difficult to get around quickly because of *the* ~~a~~ traffic. When walking down the crowded street, it's easy for a person to lose ~~the~~ *his* wallet to a pickpocket if he's not careful. There is also a lot of pollution in a big city. On the other hand, there are many fun things to do in a city. In Chicago, for example, you can

go to the top of *the* ~~a~~ Sears Tower. In Washington, D.C., you can visit *the* Smithsonian Institution. In Detroit, you can see ~~the~~ *a* baseball game at Comerica Park. Then, after *the* game, you can have dinner at the Hard Rock Café. In New York City, you can eat ~~a~~ good food at a neighborhood deli. For me, the advantages of living in a big city outweigh the disadvantages.

Exercise 9 (p. 43)

Answers will vary.

CHAPTER 8   QUANTIFIERS

Exercise 1 (p. 44)

(A lot of) people have been asking us why they should choose *SuperMegaTech* when a few cut-rate companies are offering communication services for about ten dollars less per month. That's an excellent question, and we have the answer for you: *SuperMegaTech* is simply the best value out there. We are equipped to take care of (all of) your personal communication needs. (None of) the other companies has a network as good as ours and our customer service can't be beat. We treat each customer like somebody special and (almost all of) our customers report that they are "very satisfied" with both our network and our customer service.

Our Internet service is rarely interrupted and the majority of the problems that do occur are repaired within one hour. We consider (every) Internet interruption to be an emergency. This year, (most) customers who left *SuperMegaTech* returned to our company within two months because they had experienced (more) problems with the new cut-rate companies. The other companies have neither better quality nor better customer service. They just can't offer what we do: the best of both worlds! (Most) people who try *SuperMegaTech* realize that our superb service is worth a few dollars more each month. For a limited time only, we are offering your first month of personal Internet service at a 50% discount. So try us and see why (more) people are switching to *SuperMegaTech* every day!

3. b

Exercise 2(p. 45)

2. A few   6. or
3. either   7. any
4. Some of   8. every
5. much

Exercise 3 (p. 45)

A. 2. –   4. –
    3. of
B. 1. –   3. –
    2. –   4. of
C. 1. –   3. of
    2. of   4. –

Exercise 4 (p. 45)

2. S
3. D
   Not many people were using e-mail in the early 1980s.
4. D
   All customers are important.
5. S
6. D
   A lot of people saw our advertisement.
7. D
   I like neither e-mail nor my cell phone.
8. S

Exercise 5 (p. 46)

2. b	5. a	8. b
3. b	6. a	9. b
4. b	7. b	10. a

Exercise 6 (p. 47)

A. Answers will vary. Some examples are:
   2. Most people have an e-mail account.
   3. Few people primarily communicate with their families by e-mail.
   4. Quite a few people use the computer at least once a week.
   5. Some people use computers for personal use only.
   6. Not many people use computers for business only.
   7. Almost all people have used a computer.
   8. Some computer users use only the Internet and word processing software.

B. Answers will vary.

Exercise 7 (p. 48)

2. P	5. P	8. N
3. N	6. N	9. P
4. N	7. P	10. P

Exercise 8 (p. 48)

Lori: Hey Kenny, can I use your computer later today?

Kenny: I don't know. I have a ~~lots~~ *lot* of work to do today. How much do you have to do?

Lori: Oh, I don't have a very large ~~number~~ *amount* of work to do. I only need it for a little while.

Kenny: Why don't you use a computer lab on campus? Most of ^*the* buildings have a computer lab.

Lori: I know. My dorm has two, but neither one ~~isn't~~ *is* open today.

Kenny: Neither computer lab ~~are~~ *is* open? That's weird. Are you sure?

Lori: Yes, I'm sure. I spend quite a ~~few~~ *lot of* time there. Most ^*of* the time they work fine, but ~~much~~ *most/many* computers were infected with a virus yesterday, so the labs are closed today.

Kenny: Oh, that's too bad. How ~~many~~ *much* time will it take you to finish your work?

Lori: Only about twenty minutes. I already finished the majority of it.

Kenny: I think you can use my roommate's computer. I have a lot of homework but I don't think he has ~~none~~ *any*.

Lori: Thank you so much! I'll come by later.

Exercise 9 (p. 49)

Answers will vary.

CHAPTER 9   GERUNDS AND INFINITIVES

Exercise 1 (p. 50)

I don't like (to work) late every day. I don't like my employees <u>working</u> late every day, either. Unfortunately, it will be necessary for everyone (to pitch in) and work overtime during the month of November. Our company's workload is at an all-time high, and it will continue (to increase) throughout next month. We will hire three new employees by the end of November, but in the meantime everyone will need (to pull) together in order (to ensure) that our company standards are maintained. Of course, <u>working</u> late all month will be a burden on you and your families. I understand that and I want you (to know) that I appreciate your dedication to this company. That is why all employees will receive an extra thousand dollars in their holiday bonus checks. This extra money is your compensation for <u>dedicating</u> so much time to your job this year. This company has grown very quickly over the past five years. I recognize that without you, we would not be a success. I believe that by <u>caring</u> for our employees, we will create a happy and productive workplace. I will expect you all (to work) hard this next month. However, <u>making</u> this work pleasant will be my top priority. For this reason, I also plan (to provide) food for those who stay late. Thank you all for <u>agreeing</u> (to work) overtime next month.

3. a. I
   b. my employees
   c. everyone

Exercise 2 (p. 51)

2. going	8. to quit
3. finding	9. to do
4. to make	10. to help
5. to complete	11. to get
6. eating	12. worrying
7. finding	

Exercise 3 (p. 51)

2. to buy, F	7. to know, T
3. to enforce, T	8. eating, T
4. to do, F	9. to laugh, T
5. working, T	10. to hear, T
6. bragging, F	

Exercise 4 (p. 52)

A. 2. Talking on the phone.
   3. writing an essay for History 430
   4. to speak Spanish

5. jogging in the park
6. smoking
  B. Answers will vary.
  C. Answers will vary.

Exercise 5 (p. 52)

  2. a. 2
     b. 1
  3. a. 1
     b. 2
  4. a. 2
     b. 1

Exercise 6 (p. 53)

  A. 2 Doing yoga, S
     3. to take that class, SC
     4. dancing, SC
     5. Training, S
  B. 2. to give everyone a raise, OV
     3. working too hard, OP
     4. reading aloud, OP
     5. to finish the project, OV

Exercise 7 (p. 53)

  2. This report needs finishing/to be finished.
  3. We enjoy being asked for our advice.
  4. Ron prefers being given detailed instructions.
  5. A new network has to be installed immediately.

Exercise 8 (p. 53)

  2. a. ✓   5. a. –
     b. –   b. ✓
  3. a. ✓   6. a. ✓
     b. ✓   b. –
  4. a. ✓
     b. ✓

Exercise 9 (p. 54)

Dear Nancy,

    I have a problem and I'm hoping you can help me decide what ~~doing~~ *to do*. My job has been very demanding lately and my husband has been unhappy because I've been working so much overtime. I don't mind working so much because I really like my job, but I do feel very tired after ~~to work~~ *working* so many long hours. My husband wants me to work less and I agreed to stop ~~to accept~~ *accepting* overtime assignments this month. The problem is that now my boss is requiring every employee to work overtime for the whole month of November. He is giving us an extra large holiday bonus, but my husband is very unhappy. He wants me to quit my job, but working ~~are~~ *is* very important to me. What should I do?

Sincerely,

Confused

Dear Confused,

    It sounds as if you are stuck between a rock and a hard place. You like working and ~~to spend~~ *spending* time with your colleagues, but you also like having a happy home. You shouldn't quit ~~to work~~ *working*, but you need to find a solution. First, it is essential to talk to your husband. He probably does not ~~you want~~ *want you* to be fired or reprimanded at work. He just wants ~~spending~~ *to spend* more time with you. You can make your situation at home better by ~~to talk~~ *talking* to your husband and telling him that you understand how he feels. You can let him know that you want to spend time with him, but that your job is very important to you as well. You must also talk to your boss. It is important to let him know that you are unhappy about ~~being not~~ *not being* given a choice regarding the overtime hours in November. Maybe his plan is to require the overtime now and ~~gives~~ *give* extra time off in January, for example. By talking with your boss, there may be a chance to compromise.

Sincerely,

Nancy

Exercise 10 (p. 55)

Answers will vary.

CHAPTER 10   RELATIVE CLAUSES AND ADJECTIVE PHRASES

Exercise 1 (p. 58)

    Leonardo da Vinci was a man ★(who personified) (the Italian Renaissance.) The Renaissance, ✓(which took) (place in the 15th and 16th centuries), was a time of great creativity and invention. You may have heard the term "renaissance man." A renaissance man is someone ★(who has many different skills and seems to be able to) (do anything well.) Leonardo da Vinci is a great example of a renaissance man.

    Da Vinci was an artist, writer, scientist, and inventor. He was a brilliant man ★(whose ideas were far ahead) (of his time.) In fact, some people have even suggested ★(he was an alien!) He probably wasn't an alien, but he did make detailed drawings of things ★(that we think of) (as modern inventions.) For example, he drew plans for a helicopter and for contact lenses in a time ★(when there) (was no electricity or plastic.) Of course, these items were not produced until centuries after his death.

    Most people today recognize Leonardo da Vinci mainly for his artwork. He painted *The Last Supper* fresco in Milan, as well as many famous portraits. His most famous painting is the *Mona Lisa*, ✓(which now hangs in the) (Louvre in Paris.)

Exercise 2 (p. 59)

2. Thomas Edison was the man <u>who invented the light bulb</u>.

3. That was the movie <u>(that) we saw last year</u> that was so terrible.

4. I just got a brochure for the car <u>(that) I want to buy</u>.

5. Why don't we go see the exhibit <u>(that) you are so interested in</u>?

6. Seattle is the city <u>that is famous for its coffee</u>.

7. My boyfriend found the birthday present <u>(that) I hid under the couch</u>!

8. Lori is the lady <u>(that) you met</u> <u>who I went to high school with</u>.

Exercise 3 (p. 59)

2. who/that
3. who
4. which/that
5. that/Ø
6. Ø/that/which
7. whose
8. who
9. that
10. where

Exercise 4 (p. 59)

2. work
3. give
4. was
5. are
6. played
7. we heard about
8. sees
9. she didn't cook
10. tasted

Exercise 5 (p. 60)

2. 1977 was the year <u>when Elvis died</u>.

3. Let's talk about the reason <u>why you are here</u>.

4. Willie Perdomo, <u>who is a famous poet</u>, spoke at our school.

5. Patrick is interested in dating the girl <u>who sits in the front row</u>.

6. Buenos Aires, <u>where I spent my childhood</u>, is a beautiful city.

7. Would you like some of the cookies <u>that I baked</u>?

8. Jimmy is working with Ali, <u>whose brother attends my church</u>.

9. *Catch-22*, <u>which is my favorite book</u>, was written by Joseph Heller.

10. What do you think about the paper <u>that I wrote</u>?

Exercise 6 (p. 60)

2. Rosa and Paul, who moved into our neighborhood last week, are coming to the party.
3. Veronica, who is married to a baseball player, said she can get us tickets to the game.
4. My friends met a woman who escaped the *Titanic* in a lifeboat.
5. We finally saw the movie that you told us to see.
6. Anna Maria can't go until Saturday, when she doesn't have to work.
7. I really like the book that Linda wrote.

Exercise 7 (p. 61)

2. S	4. S	6. S	8. D
3. S	5. D	7. D	

Exercise 8 (p. 61)

2. The oysters served in this restaurant made many people sick.
3. Not possible
4. Manette Edwards, my coworker, just got married in Las Vegas.
5. Not possible
6. A box weighing twenty pounds fell on my foot.
7. Not possible
8. Sorry I'm late. I stopped to help someone having car problems.

Exercise 9 (p. 62)

You all know Brandy Jones for her many wonderful inventions that <del>has</del> *have* made parenting so much easier. Last month our magazine printed an article titled, *Oh, Baby!*, ^*that/which* praised Ms. Jones' latest invention—an easy-to-use car seat for infants. This month, I had a chance to sit down with Ms. Jones, whose inventions <del>has</del> *have* revolutionized our lives.

Reporter: I can't believe I'm sitting here with the woman who invented the best car seat ever made! I love your new car seat, but that's not even the invention <del>you're most famous</del> *for which* _you're the most famous_.

Ms. Jones: Thank you so much. You're right. The invention ^*that/which* is most popular is probably the SuperFast Stroller.

Reporter: Absolutely! How do you come up with your ideas?

Ms. Jones: Whenever I see mothers <del>seeming</del> *who seem* stressed out, I wonder about the reason <del>which</del> *why* they look that way. I wonder what I can do to help. I remember feeling so stressed out in the early 1980s, when my children were still very young. That was about the time when I invented my stroller, <del>who</del> *which* was like nothing I had seen in the stores.

Exercise 10 (p. 62)

Answers will vary.

CHAPTER 10   COORDINATING CONJUNCTIONS AND TRANSITIONS

Exercise 1 (p. 63)

It seems as if happiness is hard to find these days. Everyone is looking for it, (but) very few people seem to have actually found it. Many people expect to find happiness in the world around them, (so) they search for money, power, (and) fame to make them happy. If we look at modern day celebrities, <u>however</u>, we can see that these things do not bring happiness. <u>In fact</u>, as the tabloids tell us, they often bring considerable unhappiness (and) pain. Why, then, do so many people continue to see wealth, power, (and) fame as the key to contentment?

The latest research, <u>on the other hand</u>, presents a different view of happiness. It suggests that the best way to be happier is to look within ourselves (and) try to change our behavior. <u>More specifically</u>, we need to cultivate gratitude (and) forgiveness. Studies show that people who work to strengthen these two feelings report more contentment in their daily lives. <u>Moreover</u>, people who find it difficult to forgive others have a much higher rate of heart disease. Researchers suggest, <u>therefore</u>, that everyone look for ways to be more grateful (and) forgiving. <u>For example</u>, we can all spend time each evening thinking about the positive events of the day, (so) we can feel more grateful for the good things in our lives. We can practice forgiveness by ignoring the small transgressions of others. <u>For instance</u>, if a driver cuts us off in traffic, we can choose to let it go rather than get upset. If we practice this in such instances, we might find it easier to forgive someone for a more serious offense. Practicing gratitude (and) forgiveness is good for us (and) great for society as a whole!

3. a. ✓   c. - ?
    b. ✓   d. ✓

Exercise 2 (p. 64)

2. Moreover   5. Similarly
3. In spite of this   6. and
4. or

Exercise 3 (p. 64)

A. 2. b   4. c   6. a
     3. a   5. b
B. 2. b   4. c   6. b
     3. a   5. c

Exercise 4 (p. 65)

2. S
3. D
   Lions travel in groups. Wolves, in contrast, travel alone.
4. D
   The movie was interesting, though it was too long.
5. D
   Some animals can be more dangerous than they appear. For example, many people are killed by hippos each year.
6. S

Exercise 5 (p. 65)

2. Miranda apologized, but Frank didn't care.
3. We ate dinner in a nice restaurant and saw a funny movie.
4. We arrived at the meeting late, so we had to sit on the back row.
5. The birds were flying through the air and making a lot of noise.
6. Did he call you, or did you call him?

Exercise 6 (p. 66)

Answers will vary. Some examples are:
2. Many baseball players come from Latin America. For example/instance, Sammy Sosa is from the Dominican Republic.
3. Bob stole money from his employer. Therefore/As a result, he was fired.
4. Roberta does not like children at all. As a result/Therefore, she refuses to go to a party if she knows there will be children there.
5. Our conflict resolution training can make your workplace more pleasant; additionally/in addition, it can improve your productivity.
6. Mr. Johnson is not stingy at all. On the contrary, he is the most generous man in the neighborhood.

Exercise 7 (p. 66)

2. b   4. b   6. b
3. a   5. b

Exercise 8 (p. 67)

I am disappointed to be receiving so many reports of serious conflicts amongst the employees of this company. I have worked as the human resources director for many years, ~~for~~ *and* it is my job to handle such complaints. ~~Similarly,~~ *In addition* I have never seen this many complaints in any one three-month period. ~~I~~ *On the contrary, / In contrast,* usually receive very, ~~on the contrary,~~ few reports of workplace conflict. Our company has been an enjoyable place to work for over a decade, ~~however,~~ *; however / . However* the past three months have been much different. The prospect of losing jobs is scary, but I want you to know that the downsizing is just a rumor, ~~though.~~ ~~Our, in fact,~~ *In fact, our* new CEO has promised us that there will be no downsizing for at least one full year. Your jobs are all safe*;* ~~,~~moreover, ~~and~~ everyone will be receiving a raise in January. Thank you for your hard work.

Exercise 9 (p. 67)

Answers will vary.

CHAPTER 12   ADVERB CLAUSES AND ADVERB PHRASES

Exercise 1 (p. 68)

Adverb clauses: since Mt. Fuji is an active volcano with rather unpredictable weather; in order to maintain their balance and aid in the climb; so that they will be prepared for the unpredictable weather; because the temperature can be very cold near the top of the mountain
Adverb phrases: Although climbing this mountain is quite difficult; while attempting to climb the mountain; Though difficult

Exercise 2 (p. 69)

2. By the time
3. until
4. anywhere
5. Although
6. in order to
7. because
8. though

Exercise 3 (p. 69)

2. 're repairing/repair
3. could/can
4. make
5. knew
6. gets
7. heard/had heard
8. have

Exercise 4 (p. 69)

2. Lori is learning to meditate to reduce her anxiety.
3. My brothers have visited the Metropolitan Museum of Art ten times since moving to New York City.
4. Having never met Maria's new boyfriend, we were surprised to hear they had gotten engaged.
5. Though eating healthier food, she is still having a hard time losing weight.
6. While eating dinner, we can talk seriously about moving.
7. Not possible.

Exercise 5 (p. 70)

2. D
3. D
4. D
5. S
6. S
7. D
8. S

Exercise 6 (p. 70)

Answers will vary. Some examples are:

I studied a lot for the exam so that I wouldn't be nervous on exam day.

They were working on their homework yesterday because they wanted to finish the assignment early.

You have learned so many new words while listening to the radio.

Carina called to say she'll be late since there's a lot of traffic on the highway.

I painted the walls myself so that I could save some money.

We are going to the mall because they are having a sale.

Exercise 7 (p. 71)

2. a   while touring the museum
3. b   Not knowing how to fix the sink
4. c   Though not very practical
5. a   Since watching that movie
6. b   Being so tired

Exercise 8 (p. 71)

Dear Dr. Morales,

Can you please tell me what a panic attack is? I've been having some strange feelings ~~although~~ *since* I was in a car accident last month. My sister thinks I may be having panic attacks. ~~Because~~ *because* this never happened before the accident. What should I do?

Sincerely,

Matt

Dear Matt,

Panic attacks are a type of anxiety disorder affecting millions of Americans. ~~Because having~~ *Having* had panic attacks myself in the past, I am quite familiar with them. Panic disorder is genetic, but many people begin experiencing symptoms, only after they live through a traumatic event. Panic attacks can occur anywhere the sufferer may be ~~wherever~~. Some people even have panic attacks ~~as driving~~ *while driving./driving.* Though panic attacks are scary, they are not deadly. People with panic attacks may avoid leaving their homes in order ~~to~~ avoid embarrassment. Panic attack sufferers often feel hopeless, but panic attacks can be treated with medicine and/or therapy. I hope you will see your doctor for diagnosis as soon as you ~~will~~ read this article.

Good luck!

Dr. Morales

Exercise 9 (p. 72)

Answers will vary.

CHAPTER 13   CONDITIONALS

Exercise 1 (p. 75)

Reporter: Mr. Adams, we've just received reports that you've officially announced your candidacy for mayor. Is that correct?

Mr. Adams: Yes, it is. I hope to be elected as this city's mayor in November.

Reporter: How would this city change if you were elected mayor?

Mr. Adams: Well, if elected, my first priority would be to reduce crime in the city. I would increase the city's police force by 10 percent.

Reporter: Unless you raise taxes, that will be impossible to pay for.

Mr. Adams: Well, safety is very important. Even if I have to raise taxes, I will protect the residents of our city.

Reporter: I see. What else do you want us to know about your policies?

Mr. Adams: Well, I will implement several environmentally friendly policies to reduce pollution in our city. This is urgent and it will require the cooperation of all citizens.

Reporter: What do you mean by that?

Mr. Adams: If every citizen helps out just a little bit, we will greatly reduce pollution in our city. These measures are long overdue. If more environmentally friendly policies had been implemented just fifteen years ago, we would have a much cleaner city today.

2. 3
3. a, b

Exercise 2 (p. 76)

1. c	3. d	5. b
2. f	4. a	6. e

Exercise 3 (p. 76)

2. a, b	4. b	6. b	8. a
3. c	5. b	7. b	

Exercise 4 (p. 77)

Answers will vary. Some examples are:
2. I would have given Bob some money if I had had some.
3. If you had studied more in high school, you wouldn't need to study so much now.
4. If your neighbors had seen the robber, they would have called the police.
5. If Rosa had told us she was having a problem with her workload, we could have helped.
6. If you had gone to the game, then you would have had to buy expensive tickets.

Exercise 5 (p. 77)

Answers will vary. Some examples are:
2. If I had more time, I could keep in touch with my friends more often.
3. If I had a problem with one of my classmates, I would try to talk to them about it.
4. I would get so mad if I didn't pass the exams.
5. If I were better at math, I would study engineering instead of art history.
6. If I were you, I might start preparing a resume.
7. Our noisy neighbors wouldn't bother us so much if the walls in our building were thicker.

Exercise 6 (p. 77)

1. b	3. a	5. a	7. a
2. a	4. b	6. a	

Exercise 7 (p. 78)

Dear Randall,

I am having a problem with my astronomy class this semester. If you could help me decide what to do~~,~~ I would really appreciate it. I overslept and missed the first test. Then I got a bad grade on the second test. ~~When~~ *If* I had studied, I would have gotten a good grade. I totally forgot to study, though. There are still three tests left in the class. I think I could get a C if I ~~will~~ stay in the class. If I drop the class, I won't ~~got~~ *get* a grade on my transcript at all. I am a sophomore and I have gotten either an A or a B in all my other classes. What would you do if you ~~was~~ *were* me? Would you drop the class or just try to do better for the rest of the semester?

– Oops in Astronomy

Dear Oops,

First of all, if you ~~will~~ *had* set your alarm clock, you would have made it to your first test. And if you had written your exam dates on a calendar, ~~You~~ *you* might have remembered to study for your second test. If I were you~~,~~ I would learn to be more organized and responsible. I would also take fewer classes so I could concentrate better on each class. If I were in the exact situation you are in right now, I would ~~have dropped~~ *drop* the class and try again next semester.

– Randall

Exercise 8 (p. 79)

Answers will vary.

CHAPTER 14   NOUN CLAUSES

Exercise 1 (p. 80)

In the late 1940s, several research scientists in Kalamazoo, Michigan, decided (that they wanted to create a new residential development) They quickly agreed to hire the famous architect Frank Lloyd Wright, but they had more difficulty choosing <u>where they should build their new community</u>.

By this time, Wright had already designed many of his most famous buildings, such as his Prairie houses, the Solomon R. Guggenheim Museum, and the masterpiece Fallingwater. During the Great Depression in the 1930s, he had become interested in planning communities and designing affordable houses. He believed (that affordable houses should have a style all their own) rather than being smaller copies of more expensive homes. He designed houses with a few large rooms instead of many smaller rooms. These houses encouraged more casual living, as they did not contain formal dining rooms or parlors.

The Kalamazoo group liked Wright's philosophy and after contacting him, they found a parcel of land about 10 miles from Kalamazoo. Some of the group members decided (that they would like to build the neighborhood there), but others thought (that it was too far from the city.) They decided to create two separate communities, one in this location and another just outside the city limits. This way the families could choose <u>whether they wanted to live near town or in the country</u>. Wright came to see <u>where his clients wanted their communities</u>, and he was pleased with the land they had chosen. The first community became known as Galesburg Acres and the other became known as Parkwyn Village. Wright designed the site plan for both communities, as well as four of the homes in each community. Thanks to the innovative vision of a group of 1940s professionals, the Kalamazoo area now boasts a unique collection of Frank Lloyd Wright architecture and community planning.

Exercise 2 (p. 81)

2. c	4. c	6. b	8. c
3. a	5. b	7. a	

Exercise 3 (p. 81)

A.
1. that/Ø
2. that
3. whether
4. how

B.
1. when
2. what
3. when

Exercise 4 (p. 81)

2. Everyone believed that interest rates were going to rise this year.
3. It is important that you learn to change a tire on your car all by yourself.
4. It really doesn't matter whether (or not) her friends like the new house she has chosen to buy.
5. The problem was that the family didn't have enough money to pay for Mr. Smith's medical care.
6. We should probably listen to what our boss said in the voicemail message.
7. I want to leave when you're leaving.
8. It was surprising that the children wanted to leave the beach before the adults did.

Exercise 5 (p. 82)

A. Answers will vary.
2. 7% of homeowners know if/whether their home has increased in value this year.
3. 12% of homeowners know if/ whether they will buy a new home this year.
4. 61% of homeowners know that they will not buy a new home this year.
5. 23% of homeowners don't know who has moved into their neighborhood this year.
6. 4% of homeowners have not decided where they will retire this year.
7. 58% of homeowners don't know what the crime rate is in their neighborhood.
8. 2% of homeowners aren't sure when they will retire.

B. Answers will vary.

Exercise 6 (p. 83)

2. I can't decide what to eat for dinner!
3. Not possible.
4. I'm asking you to put my car in the garage so it doesn't get damaged during the storm.
5. It is essential for students to arrive on time.
6. Not possible
7. I was thinking about how to tell you the news.
8. We are having a big debate in our family about when to take our vacation this year.

Exercise 7 (p. 84)

Dear Lola,

I have been going out with my boyfriend for three years. The other day he told me ~~what~~ *that* he wants to move to Utah to pursue rock climbing. He says he is going to move whether I ~~went~~ *go* with him or not. I don't want to move to Utah, but I can't imagine *what* ∧ my life would be like without him. I don't know why ~~would he~~ *he would* want to go without me. Maybe I did something wrong. Do you think I should move to Utah or stay where I am?

- Confused in Chicago

Dear Confused,

I understand ~~)(~~ that you really care for your boyfriend, but I don't think ~~whether~~ he is serious about your relationship. You may wonder why he wants to move, but it's not worth the trouble. Please don't waste time trying to figure ~~)(~~ out what you did wrong. This is his decision and it's not your fault. I suggest that you *stay* ~~are staying~~ where you feel more comfortable ~~there~~.

Exercise 8 (p. 84)

Answers will vary.

CHAPTER 15   REPORTED SPEECH

Exercise 1 (p. 85)

Captain Marcus Johnson of the Maysville Police Department will be retiring this fall after 35 years on the job. According to Mayor Rivera, ("the captain has done more than his share to combat crime in the greater Maysville area.") I had a chance to sit down with Captain Johnson and ask him about his distinguished career. When asked what the best part of his career was, the <u>captain smiled and said he enjoyed meeting so many wonderful people along the way.</u> <u>He explained that he felt fulfilled every time he had a chance to help a youngster avoid a life of crime.</u> <u>He also stated that his coworkers made every day of work a pleasure.</u> ("When you're part of such a dynamic team, you can't go wrong,") he said. Of course, fighting crime in our city can't always be a walk in the park. When asked about the most frustrating aspect of his job, <u>Captain Johnson answered that it was the dishonesty.</u> <u>He said it was very disappointing to see how many people would lie for any reason at all.</u> <u>The captain claimed that people could be happier if they learned to tell the truth.</u> <u>He told me that people would lie to get out of a traffic tickets, to hide the crimes of others, or to get themselves out of trouble.</u> <u>He added that the most disturbing cases were those in which a person would lie for no reason at all.</u> ("All those lies sure did make it difficult to get the) (job done.") Luckily for Maysville, Captain Johnson did get the job done during his long career. Let's hope his replacement can live up to his standards.

3. b

Exercise 2 (p. 86)

2. b, d	4. b, d	6. a	8. b, c
3. a	5. b, c	7. a	

Exercise 3 (p. 87)

2. c	4. d	6. a
3. f	5. b	

Exercise 4 (p. 87)

2. "I'll help you with your homework."
3. "You have to help me clean the house."
4. "I admit that I cheated on the exam."
5. "I'll fix the car later."
6. "The students used to turn in plagiarized papers."
7. "You should tell the truth."
8. "How long did you study for the exam?"

Exercise 5 (p. 88)

1. suggested	6. advised
2. to ask	7. told
3. insisted	8. said
4. assured	9. requesting
5. promised	10. asked

Exercise 6 (p. 88)

Answers will vary. Some examples are:
2. Paco said he probably couldn't come because he would be very busy.
3. Vera asked Paco why he was so busy.
4. Paco said he was working on the budget.
5. Vera insisted that Paco came.
6. Paco wondered why Vera wanted him there.
7. Vera told Paco that she wanted to discuss expanding the department and that she needed his support.
8. Paco asked what time the meeting was.
9. Vera told him that it was at 3:30 that afternoon.
10. Paco promised he'd be there.

Exercise 7 (p. 89)

1. I	4. they
2. his	5. my
3. him	6. we

Exercise 8 (p. 89)

Today I interviewed a group of college students who spent their spring break exploring an ice age cave in Missouri that was accidentally found by construction workers several years back. The students ~~told~~ *said* that they had ~~sign~~ *signed* up for this ten-day experience for a number of different reasons. Some ~~said~~ *told* me that they were looking for something different to do besides partying during spring break. A few mentioned that ~~we~~ *they* had read about the famous cave in the newspaper and wanted to learn more about it for ~~ourselves~~ *themselves*. Others wanted to find out if

paleontology was an interesting major. No matter what their reasons, the students reported ~~what~~ *that* they certainly were not disappointed.

In fact, their team leader said they even ~~make~~ *made* some important discoveries in the cave. She explained that the group had found a large number of microfossils dating back almost a million years and they ~~also find~~ *had found* some tracks in the clay, presumably of large cats. She ~~informed~~ *said* that these findings and others have raised a number of interesting questions for further research. For example, experts were wondering ~~does~~ *if / whether* the claw print in the cave ~~belong~~ *belonged* to the largest bear species ever to walk the earth.

Exercise 9 (p. 90)

Answers will vary.

KEY TO CHAPTER REVIEWS

REVIEW 1–3 (P. 19–20)

A.
1. c	5. c	9. b	13. a
2. a	6. a	10. a	14. b
3. c	7. b	11. b	
4. b	8. c	12. c	

B.
15. 'm visiting
16. had started/started
17. don't understand
18. 've been working
19. didn't pay
20. have you been doing/have you done/are you doing
21. is going to announce/will announce/is announcing
22. lands
23. will help/is going to help/is helping/helped
24. has she known
25. were trying

C.
26. How old will you be in 2035?
27. You say you love me, but I don't believe you.
28. We're going to win the game tomorrow./We'll win the game tomorrow.
29. I haven't smoked a cigarette since last March.
30. Please finish the report before you go home tonight.

REVIEW 4–6 (P. 37–38)

Answers will vary.
A.
1. All employees must/have got to attend the annual general meeting.
2. You should have seen a doctor about your headaches.
3. You must/have got to quit smoking.
4. You didn't have to buy me flowers.
5. Everyone should/is supposed to complete the assignment.
6. He ought to have told me he was allergic to peanuts!
7. You couldn't use cell phones in the hospital, so I went outside.
8. It may not snow tomorrow.

9. Steph can't be out. I just spoke with her!
10. You could be right this time.
B. 11. The professor was asked a question./A question was asked by the professor.
12. This color doesn't suit me.
13. ✓
14. The college library is being cleaned tomorrow so we can't use it.
15. ✓
16. I've already told you I agree with you.
17. ✓
18. My apartment is located downtown.
19. ✓
20. Has the confirmation letter been sent yet?
C. 21. a bus schedule
22. can't be rewritten
23. a geography book
24. chicken soup
25. can't be rewritten
26. a bookstore
27. junk food
28. can't be rewritten
29. cornflakes
30. can't be rewritten
D. 31. a small short-eared rabbit
32. leather hiking boots
33. an old black-and-white movie
34. a delicate Chinese vase
35. a large metal sculpture

REVIEW 7–9 (P. 56–57)

A. 1. Your bag is in the kitchen and please don't forget to take **the** laptop today!
2. ~~The~~ Love at first sight is **a** totally ridiculous idea.
3. Susan, could you feed **the** dog, please? Poor Dunbar looks hungry.
4. The car I want costs **a** thousand dollars more than I can afford.
5. I can recommend **a** great restaurant in Rome. It's right on **the** river.
6. Let me give you **a** piece of advice – never chase a lion.
7. You'll find the bank on **the** left just past **a** store called SmartMart.
8. That's weird! There are ~~a~~ policemen in your apartment.
9. Do you want chicken, ~~the~~ beef, or ~~a~~ fish for dinner tonight?
10. Ryoko had **an** awful headache so she left the office and went home.
B. 11. b, d   14. b, d   17. b, c
12. b, c   15. a   18. a, c, d
13. b   16. a, b, c, d
C. 19. having   25. to present
20. finding   26. to say
21. to get   27. Bob's
22. seeing   28. helping
23. to buy   29. calling
24. to pass   30. to come back

REVIEW 10–12 (P. 73–74)

A. 1. There are office policies which you are expected to adhere to./There are office policies to which you are expected to adhere.
2. The dog really did eat my homework, which is ironic.
3. Astronomy is a science that many people are fascinated by./Astronomy is a science by which many people are fascinated.
4. Jazz and theatre are two forms or entertainment that/which I enjoy.
5. Phil's fortieth birthday was an event (that/which) he was dreading.
6. Animal testing is an issue that many of my friends are concerned about./Animal testing is an issue about which many of my friends are concerned.
7. My grandmother, who was 98 when she died, was born in India./My grandmother, who was born in India, was 98 when she died.
8. That's the guy whose name I can never remember.
9. The package hasn't arrived yet, which means I'll be late getting home.
10. My brother was supposed to call me but he didn't, which was annoying.
B. 11. The company uses an accounting system developed in the UK.
12. There was a police announcement ordering everyone to evacuate the building.
13. A rabbit weighing 60 pounds made it into the Guinness World Records.
14. Jack, knowing there was a problem, took action immediately.
15. Anyone reading the article will know it's nonsense.
16. A system allowing tests to be generated automatically is now available.
17. Only students in a full-time program will be eligible for the grant.
18. This recipe is perfect for anyone wanting a quick, light meal.
19. Patrick, my brother, works for the government.
20. No one arriving at the gate late will be allowed to board the flight.
C. 21. b   25. a   29. b   33. a
22. b   26. b   30. b   34. c
23. c   27. c   31. b
24. b   28. b   32. c

REVIEW 13–15 (P. 91)

A. 1. a   3. a   5. a
2. b   4. b   6. a
B. 7. doesn't remember/didn't remember
8. isn't
9. take
10. wouldn't
11. might/may
12. as
13. would
14. were
C. 15. I couldn't hear what the announcer said.
16. I don't know if/whether I can tell you who the new boss is.
17. We don't have enough time, which is a problem.
18. I want to hear all about where you went last night.

19. I'm not sure whether/if he loves me.
20. Grandma is still skydiving at 90, which is almost embarrassing.
D. 21. He told me he was a professional clown.
22. ✓
23. He insisted he'd called me the day before.
24. He wanted to know if I was feeling better.
25. ✓
26. Experts warned us that the polar caps were going to melt.
27. He wanted to know when I was starting/was going to start my new job.
28. ✓
29. He told me not to worry.
30. She claimed she hadn't seen him before.

NOTES